SCHOOL IS IN SESSION

JOY OJOMAKPENE IDOKO

ISBN: 978-978-926-505-3 (Limp)
978-978-926-504-3 (Cased)

First Published 2018

Designed and Printed by:
Print Doctor Africa Ltd
Plot 10 Block A Area 4 OPIC Estate,
Agbara
www.printdoctorafrica.com

Published by

100% Joy Media Productions
Email. hundredpercentjoy@gmail.com
Instagram: @100percentjoy
Twitter: @100percentjoy

DEDICATION

Dedicated to the Most High God, my Father, my Protector and my Guide, for His unconditional and immense love for me, He has kept me by his Mercy and Grace and never gave up on me.

To my beloved father, late Honourable Justice Alhassan Idoko for all the fatherly advice and life's lessons he shared with me in those special moments we spent together.

To my dearest mother Evangelist Lydia Idoko for relentlessly praying for me and supporting me.

To my beloved son Sean, who is my wake-up call, he has always been my number one fan and biggest supporter, he had always seen what I didn't even see in myself, cheering me on day in day out.

To everyone who has ever given me a hard time, said no to me, closed a door on me, let me down and been unkind to me, thank you, you have helped me find myself and have pushed me to come out of my comfort zone and bring out the best in me. God bless you.

FOREWORD

This book explains self-discovery ,the issues of and on the greatest battle field (THE MIND) traced through the journey of knowing self, through self and by self with the all too familiar and common agent OUR THOUGHTS ,a compelling read that encourages you to take a plunge into no hold barred honest and open critical step by step look and analysis of your life's journey (thus far).As you dialogue with this smooth and easy ride you can't help but to pause and look at the front of the book to see if you are dreaming and if you had not written the book yourself.

This book describes the power of the mind how it can make you or mar you but hold on not on its own but with you being on the helm of affairs consciously or unconsciously as the lead actor. It gives you a fresh look at a very broad subject yet simplified it opens you up to realize that your life and how you live is simply the result and outcome of what you believe, it is a guide for you to realize your life as a true child of God, your gifts, talents, calling and to live it as you were originally designed to do so.

The author has been able to capture and pick thoughts and experiences which are like scattered puzzle works and unending mazes and like a spider weaving it web from unseen substances she gives and present us with a beautiful finished work ,an eye opener on how to see, treat and accept yourself, a get your confidence back armor ,a see yourself as God sees you and to borrow a common slogan A YES I CAN spirit, attitude and outlook of life, it channels you on how to accept and relate with people and almost everything around you, how to make magic out of you situations and who better to use as a guinea pig but herself. She has opened our eyes to accept ourselves as we are and also to see other as they clearly are, she has successfully taken us on a ride to self-discovery and purpose.

I recommend this book as a clear demonstration of uninhibited relationship between realization to change and the ability to conform to Gods standard and blue print for life. Like I said a get your confidence back tool, a detoxifier and a must read.

Fibi Sim Tukur
A Librarian and a Theologian is a Journalist, Media Strategists, Motivational Speaker, Publicist and Women and youth activist.

TABLE OF CONTENT

DEDICATION iii
FOREWORD iv
INTRODUCTION ix

CHAPTER 1
MEETING THE REAL YOU 1

CHAPTER 2
YOU ARE WHAT YOU THINK 7

CHAPTER 3
PUSH BEYOND THE PAIN 19

CHAPTER 4
YOU HAVE GOT TO LOVE
YOURSELF FIRST 27

CHAPTER 5
WHEN YOU DREAM, ACT 37

CHAPTER 6
YOU THINK YOU' VE GOT TIME 45

CHAPTER 7
PROTECT YOUR ENERGY 49

CHAPTER 8
KNOW YOUR POISON 55

CHAPTER 9
THE COMPANY YOU KEEP 61

CHAPTER 10
IF YOU STUMBLED MAKE IT PART OF
THE DANCE 67

CHAPTER 11
SAME LIGHTS DIFFERENT LAMPS 73

CHAPTER 12
BE ORIGINAL 77

CHAPTER 13
DANCE TO YOUR OWN MUSIC 81

CHAPTER 14
MIRROR MIRROR ON THE WALL 85

CHAPTER 15
DON'T TAKE IT PERSONAL 91

CHAPTER 16
LET GO OF THE PAST 97

CHAPTER 17
THE WORDS WE SPEAK ARE LIFE 105

CHAPTER 18
IT IS BEST TO BE QUIET 111

CHAPTER 19
THE ENEMY CALLED DEBT   117

CHAPTER 20
BE A SOLUTION   125

CHAPTER 21
MAKE YOUR LIFE COUNT   131

CHAPTER 22
BE GRATEFUL ALWAYS   135

CHAPTER 23
CONQUERING YOUR FEARS AND
ACTIVATING YOUR DESTINY   139

CHAPTER 24
LIFE IS BEAUTIFUL   143

INTRODUCTION

This book I would have said it's long overdue, but knowing what I know now, I know it is coming at the perfect time. Timing has become a very integral part of my everyday life, I have learnt to observe times and seasons, I guess that was what Solomon meant in ecclesiastics when he wrote about times and seasons.

I had dreams one of which was becoming an Author, I just didn't know where and when to start. When God started opening my eyes to some home truths about human existence and life, I knew right then the things I wanted to write about, there was also the issue of procrastinating because of some form of timidity that just didn't let me unveil my true self but learning that God has not given us the spirit of fear but of boldness and sound mind, I prayed out that fear and timidity that held me back and decided to put my dreams into action, writing my first book.

I was driving out of the house one rainy afternoon and I was thinking about life and how much God has been schooling me through my experiences and I thought about other people going through the same challenges with no clue what the outcome will be, I thought to myself, if only I could just save them the trouble of going through some of this stuff full circle, if only I could let them in on some lessons life has thought me may be in some way it could be answers to whatever they are going through right now, at that point I said to myself almost out loud, "it's time to write that book". But wait! What's the title of this book? What should it be? Suddenly the Joy I know and have come to love who hasn't lost her inner child and has the ability to get elaborately artistic with her thoughts started thinking about titles that will make this her book a bestseller and then suddenly I heard that still small voice say, "it's not about you or the applaud, we are creating out of love remember", I said "yes Lord", but…", He said "no buts" , so I came back to reality and thought through it again, letting go of self finally and said "Okay Lord what is it going to be" just then He dropped the title "School's in session" in my spirit. Suddenly I had my aha moment, that's the title am looking for, that is the exact title I need, God through this title reminding me to keep it simple, I have learnt some amazing lessons in this school called life, what better way to share them and make a difference than writing them down for you to read.

Life is a school, you learn till you die but you have to keep an open mind to learn, everything we experience, everyone we meet, every challenge we encounter, everything is meant to teach us something. The challenges and pain we go through are teachers, all you have to do is pay attention to the lessons in them and these lessons always arrive when you are ready and release yourself to learn. When decision making about your life becomes your responsibility, suddenly the reality of life starts unfolding, some of us refuse to let go of the bubbles we were raised in, others embrace the reality then the schooling begins.

One of the gifts God gave us is freewill, sometimes I think about it and I know He didn't have to because He is God, He is the boss but He did because he loves us, He gave us the gift of choice but that gift comes with a cover note, which is when you make choices , you must take responsibility for your choices, It's just like writing an objective exam in school, you have options to choose from, the teacher doesn't control those choices but in the end the outcome of your answers is either a fail or a pass, which you were solely responsible for. That is life, it comes with choices, you get to choose, and you get to live with it. The good thing about life is, when you make mistakes you can learn from them and start all over again, it gives you chances, but be careful not to misuse those chances so you don't run out of chances.

Every experience we have in life whether good or bad are meant to teach us something or grow us into who we are destined to become, the best versions of ourselves. Our paths in life are tailored towards our why, why we are here. Some people have a pretty smooth sail others are off to a rocky start but an amazing finish, although our choices play a major role in all this, whatever your start, the whole idea is making sure you finish strong and truly live, leaving an indelible mark in your generation. God has laid down principles that can help us go through life the way He intended it for us, we just need to let go of what we think we know and let

Him school us through life.

I do not see myself as an authority on anything but I have been in the school of life long enough, had some experiences, struggled with some hard truths, learnt some lessons, surrendered to the highest tutelage, passed some courses with flying colours, had some carry overs, and still learning daily. Know this nothing really goes away until it has taught you what you are meant to learn, stripping you of the old you and revealing and birthing a newer and better version of you, we are all works in progress, working towards becoming master pieces just as God has created us, The chisel and the hammer is in your hands, you can either become a better you, priceless and valuable or you can remain in your raw state, like you were created for nothing. This book is meant to share those lessons I have learnt and the principles God has thought me to apply daily in life with you, you never know you just might learn a thing or two. To learn you must let go of what you think you already know and embrace growth and change, learn the lesson so you don't have to keep taking the test. You are the greatest project you will ever work on, so take your time and create a master piece. If you are ready SCHOOL IS IN SESSION.

CHAPTER
1

MEETING THE REAL YOU

"I understood myself only after I destroyed myself. And only in the process of fixing myself, did I know who I really was" ...Sade Andria Zabala

Have you ever wondered about your existence, who you really are, why you are here on this earth, what potentials you have, who you are meant to be and what you are meant to do? We were all created for a reason, none of us are here by accident, no biological mistakes, no flukes, you were destined to come on the day, hour, minute and second you came, through the union of the two exact souls you came through, God gave custody of you to your parents out of billions of choices on earth because they are the ones who are meant to play the role of building the foundation that propels you towards the destiny He has for you.

The foremost assignment in our lives is finding our real selves and discovering who we are and why we are here. The journey to self-discovery is inevitable, for you to find your purpose and fulfil it, you must go through a transformation that grows you into who God has destined you to be, this is the point when God illuminates your mind to see beyond the physical, He opens your eyes to see the world as He intended it, to understand the reason why you are here and what His plans are for you, what his plans are for humanity and your role in it, that is the journey to self-discovery, I call the process the creation process and my understanding of it came from genesis 1, it is the most important event in your life apart from your birth, the point at which you come to the awareness of who you truly are.

This revelation of the journey to self-discovery came to me when I was going through a process of re-discovering myself .When you are going through the transformation process it is very chaotic at first because the old you will fight the emergence of the new you , you wouldn't understand what you are feeling or going through at the beginning, it is all chaos and pain while on the inside a raging battle is ongoing between the old you and the emerging you, you begin to reflect the conflict going on inside you ,outside you ,through your relationships with other people, you feel like the world is against you because your new self is warring against your old self, it is a confusing and hard experience but once you give in to the process it becomes a very liberating journey, everything negative limiting you and your old ways of doing things begin to die as you begin to shed off the old you, the things that interested you in the past that do not serve your purpose will become uninteresting to you, vanity becomes repulsive to you, you begin to search for a deeper meaning to life, you begin to face yourself even more and deal with the core which is the real essence of who you truly are, you start questioning everything you grew up believing. You begin to want more out of life, you look forward to every morning with enthusiasm, you are no longer content with the regular or the ordinary, a different level of understanding of life and the world around you comes to you, you begin to want more out of life because now you know there is a higher purpose, you want to be true to who you are, you want to really understand your existence and purpose. You begin to ask yourself a lot of questions and because you are ready the answers begin to come. This journey of self-discovery going on inside of you begins to create an amazing change in your outer reality, pushing you towards a more authentic life one that doesn't give room for mediocrity and anything that is keeping you away from your true potential, you start disconnecting from wrong friendships and things that are not giving you fulfilment, you begin to align yourself with things and people that build you up and are in line with your growth. You begin to see the world differently, you become very aware of the world around you, colours, sounds, touch, feelings become more intense, it begins to feel like you understand everything, you begin to understand the why and how, you begin to walk with

God, feeling His love, understanding it and radiating the love all around you to a point where people can tell and they begin to compliment you. You hear God when he speaks to you, you hunger for a supernatural experience with God every day, you become one with everything and all that really matters is you fulfilling you purpose and being the best version of you as God intended.

When you get to this point you know that you just met the real you, you have come to a full understanding of why you are on this earth, and your days of living aimlessly groping in the dark, clueless about your life is over. Life as you should live it begins at this point. When you get to this point the question is what are you going to do with this new you? Are you going to trust your new journey and give yourself to this process of self-discovery or fall back into the old and dark place you just emerged from because you will rather stay where you are used to and comfortable in. When you do not give yourself to the process it is so easy to fall back to the old you, because it is a constant battle between the old and new you, and the you that you succumb to wins. The decision to be the best version of you is yours to make, you are a work in progress and that progress depends on the decisions you make concerning your journey.

A few years ago, I started my journey of self-discovering, it started with me questioning everything around me, I starting wanting more, more than the regular norm,

I wanted to experience God in a different way. I had so many questions about life, about the things I was taught growing up and the way I saw people live life in general, I needed so many answers, but the most troubling questions were, why we are all here, what my purpose here on earth is, why does God allow some experiences in our lives? what plans does God have for me and who really am I? This and so many other questions troubled me, I started to lose sleep at night, I became uninterested in socialising with people, I became withdrawn, so much was going on the inside of me, my mind was constantly racing, I could barely get a hold of my thoughts, I was getting a rush of answers and it became really scary, I thought I was losing my mind, I was on the verge of having a nervous breakdown, so quickly I turned to God for help, I stopped fighting it and I surrendered to Gods tutelage, at that point I began to listen and my eyes and my mind became opened to my life as God intended it , I came into the awareness of who God has created me to be, I had belittled myself for so long and underestimated my capabilities, I had lived like a servant , forgetting I was royalty and the daughter of a king, it was like home coming. For the first time God told me what I am on this earth for, what His purpose for me is, I now understood the fact that I had a role to play on this earth and no other person could be me, I am unique and here for a reason, a mission, at that point I began to truly live, life now had meaning, it doesn't happen overnight , it is a process a journey ,you must commit to, I committed to my journey and it has been a hundred percent joy from then onwards, regardless of the high and lows and whatever the journey entails. When you go through a process of self-discovery life becomes beautiful, meeting the real you will birth the purest form of love anyone can ever feel for one's self, this love you begin to radiate and show other people, the love becomes the reason for everything you do, once that emotion becomes your motivation, the sky is only the beginning , it realigns your life and gives it meaning , you begin to unleash the best version of yourself and create impacting ripples that will start a huge wave of change in your world. Until you rediscover yourself and know who you are, know your identity, nothing ever changes, you will keep going through the same circles of challenges in life until you give in to the process and journey to self-discovery. Once you meet the real you and BECOME, you have conquered self and won one of the greatest battles of your life and unlock the door to your success in life.

CHAPTER
2

YOU ARE WHAT YOU THINK

"When a flower doesn't bloom you fix the environment in which it grows, not the flower"
Unknown

The mind is the most powerful tool God has ever given man, Great writers like King Solomon, Napoleon Hill, Jack canfield, Warren buffet, Paul Coelho, Mike Murdock and a host of others have stressed the fact that our thoughts create our reality. Your mind can build or destroy you; it is your mirror and how you see yourself in your mind is how people see you in real life, whatever your mind cannot grasp you cannot achieve in the physical. If you realize how powerful your thoughts are, you would never think a negative thought in your life. Thoughts send out a frequency that vibrates into reality, in other words you attract what you think, believe it or not you are creating your own experiences.

This is one secret I wish I discovered much earlier in life before I knew fear, negative thoughts and doubt. I see this three as our greatest enemies, once your mind is filled with fear, doubt and negative thoughts it sets the tone for how your real life plays out. It is like planting weeds in your vegetable garden yourself. My biggest challenge has been my mind, and I think it is the biggest challenge for most people, because when the devil wants to cripple you , he attacks your mind first, I always tended towards thinking negative thoughts, fear of failure, fear of harm, fear of the dark, fear of rejection, fear of loss, fear of everything, I fought with these fears for years and they held me back from discovering my full potential, even when I did discover it all the negativity never really allowed me to grow into who God had destined me to be, I always thought the worst possible outcome of everything instead of the best. I will come up with great ideas and plans but I was always afraid to follow through for fear of being wrong or laughed out or even failing, so I had all these tall dreams I needed to work towards achieving but I wasn't working towards them because I had crippled my mind with my thoughts.

When you fill your mind with negative thoughts and let negative emotions take over, you are setting yourself up for failure and a life of misery. Your mind responds to what you feed it, every event in your life is first created in your mind. You mind is the canvas upon which you create your reality, how you feed it determines what you go through, if you are always thinking the worse of and for yourself that is what you will always get. Take for instance if you constantly think of the things you do not have, you will always stay in lack, if you constantly think about ill health, you will find yourself falling ill regularly, if you constantly think about being broke, you will find it manifesting in your life, if you think you are always unlucky with relationships, you will find yourself having endless failed relationships, if you think people won't like you, trust me they won't. The way you feel on a daily basis is determined by your thoughts, bad mood, foul mood or good mood all is determined by the thoughts that you let take root in your mind. It is easy for you to try to blame your foul or bad mood, disappointments, failure, debts on other people, the recession or anything else but yourself, but the hard truth is how you let those external situations play out in your mind and the thoughts you dwell on are responsible for how you feel and all that is happening to you. What you do not want, you do not dwell your thoughts on. When you focus your thoughts on all the things you do not want all you get is more and more of those things in your life. The way we handle our daily challenges and how we let it affect us is solely determined by our thoughts about them. The question is are you in control of your thoughts or your thoughts race around on their own dishing out feelings to you as it deems fit? You may not have the power to change your immediate situation but you have the power to choose the thoughts you let take root in your mind about the situation, when you think positive thoughts about how you will rather your situation was instead of dwelling on a situation you cannot control, you situations begins to improve for the better, I have heard stories of people who were confined to wheel chairs for life who are walking today , I have heard of people who have been giving 6 months to live who are still alive 15 years later, I have heard of people who beat cancer, but you see in as much as a lot of people have these testimonies, there are people who are faced with the same situations who are still in wheel chairs, who died before the 6 months call, who died from cancer, you know why ? The difference between those who beat their situations and those who did not is the thoughts they let take root in their minds, what the constantly thought about in their minds saved the prior group and destroyed the latter. My mum fell ill when I was just 11 years, I didn't know much but I know the doctors kept coming up with different diagnosis and each time the treatment wouldn't work and she kept getting worse, she was admitted in the hospital for weeks, eventually they said she had parasite of unknown origin, she was giving some drugs they said she had to take for life, she rejected everything the diagnosis, the drugs and all and asked to be discharged, the doctors said it was risky to go home, she could infect us or even lose her life, she rejected all the told her and insisted on going home, so she was discharged. The type of faith my mum exhibits is most times incomprehensible, she can see the most hopeless situation and still refused to be moved by it and insist on the best outcome possible, she dwells on it and she always gets it no matter what. She told my father she would not live on drugs for life, she said she was healed and sickness had not power over her, most people thought she was out of her mind, she turned to the only doctor I have always know her to turn to, she calls him Doctor Jesus. After a very close shave with death and a supernatural encounter she got out of her bed, never took the drugs she was given and up till today lives a very normal and healthy life. My mum is the only elderly parent I know who doesn't go for routine check-ups, eats anything and everything, doesn't have any lifestyle disease, and is still as agile as she was when I was a little girl. The only reason she has this stress-free healthy life is because of the way she thinks, she is a positive thinker, her thoughts are creating the life she is living. Most of the suffering you are experiencing is only in your thoughts and 90 percent of those things will never happen, your thoughts have made you suffer from anxiety, depression, and worry over things that will never happen, take it from someone who knows.

There was a time I used to worry so much about not having enough money to pay my bills, and guess what I was constantly in debt, sometimes when I made good money, I start worrying about running out of the money, so instead of thoughts of multiplication my thoughts were on the money depleting and guess what in a very short period all that money would be gone. I had all sorts of negative thoughts and fears and it crippled my mind to a point that I had a nervous breakdown, I thought I was losing my mind, then a dear friend of mine told me to read a book called " The Secret" by Rhonda Bryne, this book changed my whole orientation and marked a turning point in my life, my friend told me the problem was my mind, I wasn't feeding it right, he told me to change my thinking, seek God s face and help and see how different my life will be, honestly it was the beginning of the best days of my life , I could not believe I have been so self-destructive with my own thoughts for so long, I was my own worst enemy , at that point I broke down and ask God for His help and from then onward He started teaching me how to be better. Know that a negative mind finds faults in everything but a positive mind finds opportunities and possibilities in everything. I read somewhere that what you set your sights on with clear intentions is what you steer towards, it is what you draw into your life.

The truth is your mind must arrive at your destination before you do, whatever you intend to achieve your mind has to be able to create a spiritual blue print first, if it can't see it then you cannot achieve it. Your thoughts are the creative power you use to create your future. What you think you become, what you feel you attract, what you imagine you create. Everything ever invented, created or manufactured started as a thought, which means these people channelled their thoughts productively and they were able to create amazing inventions, products and services that has changed and impacted the history of human existence. What are your most predominant thoughts today? Are they thoughts of self-pity, frustration, bitterness, resentment, depression, suicide, hate and lack or are they thoughts of love, hope, peace, joy, faith, abundance and good health? Whichever thoughts you are entertaining is creating more of that situation and feelings in your life, emotions are an amazing gift God has given us, it makes us aware of what we are thinking. If you are feeling bad you will naturally go off track creating the future you desire, if you have good feelings, then you know your life is on track, change your mind set and change your life, it's all happening first in your mind, every battle in your life is first won or lost in your mind. Everything you are experiencing now your thoughts are creating them for you, if you do not like your life right now, change your thoughts, if you do not like a situation you are in, change how you are thinking and feeling about it and watch the tides turn in your favour. Be optimistic about life, being pessimistic stops you from achieving your set goals or putting yourself in the midst of opportunities. You can say all the right words and affirmations by faith by if you do not have a mental image of what we desire, if you do not shape your thoughts towards that reality you speak of and tune your feelings positively, they will remain only mere words, that is why you speak and do not see the results, or you act and you do not get results because your mind has not received the right thoughts, your thoughts are conflicting your words and actions. How can you have all the most negative thoughts running through your head about your life, your dreams, your friends, your boss, your family and your spouse and expect positive outcomes in reality. The best way to change a bad situation is to think positive thoughts about that situation, let your thoughts dwell on the outcome you want, consistently dwell on it, concretize it in your mind and watch the change happen in real life.

You can choose your thoughts, as different thoughts rush into your mind, choose to focus on positive thoughts, reject negative thoughts immediately they pop up because they will and replace it quickly with a positive thought, uproot the weed before it grows rooted in your mind. Have you noticed it is easier for you to think and assume the worse of people and situations, when you call someone and he or she doesn't pick up the phone or you sent a text , you can see it has been read and you didn't get a reply , it's easier to think , "oh this person is avoiding me", he or she is being rude, he or she doesn't want to talk to me and the more you accept those thoughts the more maybes you get , sometimes you start thinking did someone tell him or her what I said about her, your mind is all over the place processing the worse, and suddenly the person returns your call , with an apology and a very valid explanation , I have felt stupid so many times thinking and assuming the worse with people, sometimes we take a step further and act on those thoughts and create problems where there was none. This has ruined a lot of friendships, marriages and relationships, your partner is unreachable and the thoughts of infidelity begins to flood your mind, most times people act on those thoughts and begin to accuse and attack their partners in the end ruin a beautiful thing because of the thoughts you chose. You are applying for a job or going for a competition, you get there and see other applicants or competitors and immediately you begin to think you are not good enough, why would they pick you out of all this people, the interviewer or judges do not like you, these thoughts take root and you already lost out before the competition or interviews started because in your mind you already gave up and saw a hopeless situation.

When you are confronted with situations or hard times make up your mind to stay positive no matter what, always find a positive way to think about whatever situation you find yourself, this is the easiest way to turn any difficulty into an opportunity. See tough times as a learning experience that is bringing you closer and closer to achieving your dreams, be grateful for every situation good or bad, have a positive mental attitude at all times, tough times won't last for ever, but how long they last is depended on how long you let it based on your thoughts and attitude towards it.

Your feelings and attitude are dependent on your thoughts, make a conscious effort to choose positive, happy, hopeful and faith filled thoughts, choose to think good thoughts about other people, focus on the good only the good, it could be difficult given that the bad always stares right in the face. Sometimes when it's difficult to see the good, focus on the lesson and be thankful, the truth is in every bad situation there is a lesson, your attitude towards the situation will determine if you recognise the lesson and learn from it. If you have been betrayed by a friend, instead of nursing thoughts of resentment and hurt why don't you focus on being grateful for the experience that has taught you how to choose better friends and improve your relationship with others in the future?

Know this the battles of this life are not won by the strongest or the smartest but by the person who thinks and believes he or she can win. Today choose to be that person, choose to focus on thoughts that creates a better life for you. I will tell you one last story, it's about a friend of mine a young man called Uti Nwachukwu the winner of the big brother Africa all-stars edition some years back, before he went for the big brother all-stars, he was going through the worst time of his life, the buzz about his first big brother Africa journey had died down and his friends had all turned their back on him because his fame had gone cold. He fell into depression in the worse way, so much was going on in his life, there was the betrayal from friends, he was struggling with his youth service in a strange city and barely had the finances to cope with it , he dad was just diagnosed with cancer, he had reached a breaking point overwhelmed by everything he was going through, at that point he discovered the power of his thoughts through a spiritual encounter, and he began to exercise it , pray and develop a positive outlook to life, he began to envision the life he wanted and created a concrete picture of it , if you are close to Uti you will know he has always believed he will have the life he has now. We were having a conversation one day and he talked about his mistakes he made the first time he was in the big brother house and in his words he said passionately , "if I had just one chance to do this all over again I will do things differently" , fast forward a few months later , the big brother Africa all-stars edition was starting up and the interesting thing was he was not Nigeria's pick for the competition but because he was steering his thoughts in the right direction, God started putting everything in place to give him that second chance to the life he desired. The person who was meant to go for the competition turned it down and Uti was now called last minute to take his place, when he got to South Africa, he could tell he was not originally meant to be there because everything about the Nigerian contestant was tailored towards the other guy, they had to start adjusting everything to fit Uti. He got into that competition with only one thought and mind-set that he was winning that competition no matter what. Every day in the house morning and night he visualised his win, prayed about it, was grateful for it, he never let any other thought into his mind except the fact that he was the winner of the competition. Outside the house everyone was analysing and seeing the winner coming from a different country since a Nigerian won the year before and since the public vote also wasn't particularly in Uti s favour. The finale came and Uti made it to the final five, the elimination process started and the last five were ready for their fate, one after the other the house mates were called out, and the last two were Uti and Munya , I knew at that point Uti had won the competition, something was different about him this time , he had changed his attitude towards himself, towards his situation and towards people, he had replaced every negative thought with positive thoughts , he started walking with God and he was ready for the life he desired. In the end Uti was announced the winner of the competition, the confidence he exuded after the initial shock will tell you he was prepared for this outcome, today he is the most successful celebrity any reality show in Africa has produced, he is a TV presenter with Africa magic, an actor, model, artist and compere, his success has risen with every year and today he is living the life he used to dream about.

You attract your predominant thoughts, your life is a mirror of those thoughts, your draw everything you are experiencing to yourself; your life is a manifestation of your thoughts and those thoughts are shaping the world around you. You too can live your dreams the only thing holding you back is your mind set, change your mind set and your life will be transformed.

CHAPTER

3

PUSH BEYOND THE PAIN

"Stop trying to skip the struggle that is where character is built"

The first step to change is to become aware of your own bullshit, when you finally come to the realisation and accept the fact that you need to strip yourself of all that does not serve you and start taking yourself seriously, change comes and growth begins. Once you learn to accept who you truly are, you begin to grow. Change comes with growth and growth most times is painful, but for you to blossom you must push beyond the pain. Some periods of our growth are so confusing that we don't even recognise that growth is happening. We may feel inimical or angry and agitated even depressed, I am sure some of you can relate. The feeling is most times unpleasant. It is in these phases that we come to the realisation that we are being prepared for the next phase of our lives and in the process a new and improved you is unveiled.

The saying it is darkest before dawn is not just a saying it is actually darkest before dawn. With child birth, it is the most painful before the birth of your bundle of joy, the steepest part of the climb is when you are almost at the top of the mountain or hill. The toughest and most challenging part of every endeavour is just at the edge of breakthrough and sadly most of us give up just at the edge of success. A fitness instructor once told me something that has helped me keep my weight off. He says when working out, at the point when it starts getting really hard and it feels like my whole body burns and I can't go on anymore that is when I should push harder. I should push beyond that pain because that is when the fat burning starts, that is when my bodily change begins, believe me I have found that to be true and I have applied it to every aspect of my life, once I push pass the pain or difficulty, I begin to see results. We must condition our minds to push beyond the pain, that pain is growth, it is progress and it requires our final push, breakthrough always comes after the pain.

God uses the most regular occurrences around us to teach us His deep truths, well that is after we learn to listen, but that is a topic for another chapter, when I learnt to listen God started my life's training opening the eye of my mind to understanding the deep things using the most unlikely illustrations around me, and each time He does that it's like an "AHA" moment. The Illustration I am about to take you through is the birthing process, if you understand the birthing process you will understand what God expects of you during your growth process and at the edge of your breakthrough.

When a woman gets pregnant, she carries the baby most times for nine months after which she births a baby, a bundle of joy, then there is the celebration, what people do not understand is the process and what the nine months entails, same thing goes with our dreams and our journey to success. Now we have dreams God has planted in us, when we finally grow into the realisation of that dream and begin to nurture it, it begins to grow as we pursue it. When you begin to work towards that dream your gestation period begins, your nine-month season begins, it might take years, months, weeks, but know that you will always have your gestation period, your nine-month season comes before you birthing season, your success and it comes with three trimesters.

The first trimester is the time you discover your dream, your purpose, there will be lots of excitement, questions to be answered and mixed feelings that tend towards nostalgia. There might possibly be fear of the unknown because you do not know what to expect or what to do, then the morning sickness will come, it will be discouraging and uncomfortable because the growth of a new life has begun, you might want to quit but you keep going, with encouragement from your partner, family, friends and most importantly you Doctor (God) who you have placed all your trust in and you know He has got your back. Soon that stage filled with uncertainties and confusion and discomfort is over, you are now in your second trimester. Things are clearer now, your dream is gradually becoming a reality, things are taking shape, looking more rounded and visible and you are growing considerably into a better version of yourself. This is a very sensitive and crucial stage, things are looking up so you have to be extra careful, keep the right company, be careful who you share your dream with, feed your mind right with the right diet to ensure your dream is nourished properly, visit and talk to your doctor regularly through prayers and meditating on God's word, if not you stand the risk of a miscarriage. This is the stage where people would try to abort your dreams by discouraging you and instilling fear into you if you let them, if you give ear to negativity at this point you stand the danger of a miscarriage, so focus on your goal and trust God to see you through.

Now you are in the last trimester, the dream starts getting really heavy , at a point too heavy to carry , you are tired of carrying it and all you can think of is bringing it forth, some many sleepless night , nothing fits anymore , the aches , the pains but you keep focusing on the birth to come, then finally its time and the labour pain starts , life feels like hell, you have no money, no food, no help, no job, doors seems to be closed, seems like every one planned to disappoint you at the same time, looks like the world is against you, no one is meeting deadlines or keeping to commitments , you feel like giving up, but guess what you don't give up, because you can't give up now because if you do your dream dies and there is a slim chance it's the end of you too, then you try to hold on but the pain only gets worse, so unbearable you think you are going to die, trust me you are at the edge of your breakthrough about to birth something great, something that will change the course of history and affect your generation in ways you have never dreamed of, now it's time to push, now that the pain is unbearable it is time to push, it's a life or death battle now, it's now or never , you push! people who believe in you will urge you to push , you are almost there, you can do it , then there is always this one midwife who will tell you that you are disturbing the hospital with you screams , you don't pay her any attention , you push, push harder, scream if you have to , cry, bite, whatever you have to do to push that baby out , because you know that this dream must be born , it must come alive, stay focused its almost here , now you are almost out of breathe, you can barely feel your own heartbeat , you are exhausted, feels like you can't go on anymore, the baby is crowning , you just need one last push, you can't give up now, then this final sharp pain comes and you push, push so hard with all that you have got , finally the baby is born, you feel this relieve that can't be described with words, all of the sudden all the pain and tears are worth the birth of this miracle, Listen! finally that's the cry of your baby, of victory , success, accomplishment , glory , your baby is here, your dream is a reality, you change has come , like magic you can't remember the pain anymore , you have tears of joy streaming down your face, people begin to celebrate you and applaud you including the ones who didn't think you could make it, especially that midwife who was giving you a hard time, don't get carried away now, it's time to nurse that baby , the dream is now a reality and you are ready to change the world with your work, as you celebrate your birthing season , get ready to keep that dream alive , nourish it, nurture it , love it, feed it day in day out , don't even neglect it until it becomes what you had dreamt it will be.

God wants you to push beyond the pain, He allows this pain for a reason, it is part of Gods plan to wake you up and push you out of your comfort zone, so you can discover all the potentials He has put in you to take you to the successful future He has planned out for you, the pain is part of the process and there is always a message in it for you. You need to surrender yourself to the process and let it catapult you to your place of celebration. When you fill like you are been buried in your problems know that God is planting you to grow and push through that soil of your situation to bloom into a better you. Pain is one of the greatest gift God has given us, pain makes us aware of what we need to change or work on and it's our spiritual pointer to growth. You pain has a purpose and it is a process you must go through, no one prepares you for the amount of pain in your growth process, just like a mother cannot tell you how painful labour pain will be, you only know it by experiencing it and no matter how many babies you have you are never prepared for the experience. It will come, but you attitude towards the pain determines the outcome. Give yourself over to the process, feel it and let yourself go, let God take control, maintain an attitude of thanksgiving, be prepared, because after the pain comes the gain. Sometimes our lives need to be completely shaken up, changed and rearranged to reposition us in the place we are meant to be, the pain sometimes is a set up for greater things, I will tell you a story about the Hollywood actor Dwayne Johnson popularly known as 'The Rock', during his high school years, Dwayne began playing football and he soon received a full scholarship from the University of Miami, where he had tremendous success as a football player. In 1995, Dwayne suffered a back injury which cost him a place in the NFL, he didn't give up, he just pushed beyond that pain and redirected his focus and he decided to pursue a career in wrestling. He made his wrestling debut in the USWA which launched him into a very successful career in the WWE, he didn't stop there, in 2000, the Rock took time off from WWE to film his appearance in The Mummy Returns, from that moment on he has been starred in most block buster movies in Hollywood, including the viewer's choice the fast and furious, Dwayne has the ninth largest followership on Instagram with 95million followers, and is rated one of the most talented actors in Hollywood. Dwayne was able to get to this point in his life because he didn't give up, he didn't take his set back with his injury as a reason to give up on his dreams but he saw it as life giving him another route to success, today he is one of the most celebrated Hollywood actors of our time.

I heard someone say the road to success is hard but not impossible unless you think it is impossible then it will be , it's all up to you, stick it out, suffer through, show you strength, courage and perseverance, make it happen no matter what and one day they will speak of you, the world will hear of you and celebrate you, the one who didn't give up, the one who fought back and made it through, the one who stood against all odds and made it to the top, Les Brown said " you will experience some turbulence before you reach a comfortable altitude" so fasten your seat belt because it will be a bumpy ride. If you are going through a dark time right now, be encouraged by the fact that your breakthrough is almost here, get up dust yourself and own your pain, face your situation head on with the expectation of great things to come you are moving up to the next level of your life and everything you are going through is God schooling you to get you ready for greater things, let the pain grow you, don't you give up just hang in there your season of celebration is almost here.

CHAPTER
4

YOU HAVE GOT TO LOVE YOURSELF FIRST

"Self-acceptance changes things. Love yourself" ....
Kay Antoinette
"You are not required to set yourself on fire to keep
other people warm" Unknown

Loving yourself sets the tone for how you love others and how you are loved by others, when you love yourself enough to set standards people will work hard to meet those standards and love you the way you teach them to. You cannot give what you do not have, if you do not know how to love yourself, you cannot love others or reciprocate the love shown to you.

How do you treat yourself? Like a doormat that people can walk all over or an exotic island that people need to put in some good work to get to? People will treat you the way you treat yourself, if you let them walk all over you because you are so simple and too nice then you will be that door mat everyone cleans his or her leg on to step up, don't blame them, you showed them how you see yourself and how you want to be treated, but if you value and love yourself enough to walk away from anything that does not serve you, you will set a precedence for how people relate to you. You have to learn to walk away from negativity and anyone who treats you less than you deserve, when you tolerate disrespect and make excuses for people who disrespect you, it's not going to stop it will only get worse. When I began to learn to love myself, I cut ties with a lot of people I knew over the years, because by re-evaluating my relationship with them I discovered I deserved better, although I also came to terms with the fact that most of them treated me the way they did because I allowed it. People treat you the way you treat yourself, when you tend to accommodate people's excesses, they are not going to check themselves even if they know better, trust me they will take advantage of it all.

I started asking myself what self-love is, how do I love myself? For anyone to understand self-love you must understand the concept of love, love is the most powerful force on earth, to give it you must first know it and feel it within you, Jesus tells us we should love our neighbours as ourselves not more than our selves or less than, love your neighbour as if you are loving yourself, just the way you love yourself. Loving anyone at the expense of yourself is self-abuse, it shows you have little or no regard for yourself, if you don't love yourself, how do you expect someone else to love you, it is in loving yourself people will learn and know how to love you. Love is give and take, it's not give and give or take and take, if you feel you are giving of yourself to a point that it is draining you then I don't think love is in play here and you need to love yourself enough to walk away from any relationship that is patterned that way. You set the tone for how people love you. The way you love yourself will show people how you deserve to be loved. The minute you realise your worth you shift your energy to attract new people who respect your worth, it starts with you first, when you start taking care of yourself, you start feeling better you start looking better and you start attracting better. I watched a very inspiring video by some lady author titled "Dare to take". In it she admonishes women not to live by the myth that a woman is meant to keep giving and giving regardless, we need to understand that it is ok to take too, and we should dare to take. Its ok for it to be about you sometimes, you are not selfish to put your dreams first or choose to follow them, it is ok to be about you sometimes, don't let anyone make you feel guilty because you chose you, because in the end, life is short and our time here should be put into good use living out the purpose God brought us here for. Know this! You will regret the things you did not get to do because you forgot you also matter, you forgot you are priority and every second counts in fulfilling your

God given destiny.

Loving yourself means you letting go of anything that doesn't serve you, loving yourself means you choose to stripe yourself of parts of you that is stopping you from being the best version of yourself, loving yourself means you always want the best for yourself, loving yourself means you walking away from negativity and toxic relationships. You begin to focus your energy on growing yourself, your vision and your purpose, you no longer have time for drama, resentment or meaningless relationships because you now know they only deplete your energy and jeopardize your growth and purpose.

When you love yourself, you begin to take care of yourself physically by making sure you are very fit and healthy, you stop abusing your body with the wrong food, drugs, substances or immoral behaviour that will destroy it.

Emotionally you begin to protect your emotions by staying away from any relationship that is toxic to you or any relationship that your feelings, needs, dreams do not matter and you are neither seen nor heard. Know this! When you give too much importance to someone in your life at the expense of yourself you begin to lose your value in theirs.

Psychologically you begin to train your mind to think only positive thoughts and choose positive feelings that will grow you and help create the life God intended for you.

Spiritually you begin to build a relationship with God, learning to listen to Him and doing His will, you begin to search for a higher purpose and walk in that purpose to fulfil God s mandate for you on this earth.

Loving yourself means working on yourself more than anything else, you are your own masterpiece and you must chisel off the parts of you that not serve you or Gods purpose for you, take a good look at yourself ask yourself what you can improve , work on improving every part of you that is working against you , get rid of anything that will distract you from achieving your destiny or being the best version of yourself , it might be a relationship, it might be the company you keep, unhealthy habits, or too much TV, whatever it is love yourself enough to rid yourself of it. I read somewhere that "you should remember to take care of yourselves, you can't pour from an empty cup" you have nothing to give if you think you are nothing, you can't give what you don't have, if you do not love yourself, you cannot love someone else. It is only in loving yourself you can love others. Loving yourself means you stop second guessing yourself, you stop thinking there is something wrong with you, you stop feeling you are not good enough, sometimes the only thing wrong with you is your belief that som   ething is wrong with you in your mind. Our greatest enemy is our selves. Most times we fight ourselves the most, we are our own stumbling block. For the enemy outside to get to you, the enemy within must have let him in, you already set yourself up for a fall, the hardships and circumstances you face on the outside are just responding to the conditions you have created on the inside. Self-love and acceptance bring you to a point where you stop questioning yourself and your actions and you start trusting the decisions you make in your best interest. Loving yourself changes everything, you will lose friends, you will sometimes be called selfish, and you will even be taken on a guilt trip, when you let God school you, you will be able to tell the difference between self-love and selfishness, have confidence in being yourself regardless of how anyone feels about it , you shouldn't try to be someone else just to please others simply because they do not like who you are , trust me there are people out there ready to accept you for who you are, people who are ready to accept your past , present and future, your scars, your darkness and your light, people who have no desire whatsoever to change you, but are ready to love and support the very person you are and see you succeed .

When you begin to love yourself you no longer allow people abuse your time by wasting it on frivolities because you are beginning to realise how valuable you time is and respect it, believe me at first, they will despise you for it but guess what after a while they will come to respect you for it. One of the strongest enemies of self-love is the inability to say NO. Learn to say NO, when it is not convenient for you, if it is not working for you, if it doesn't serve you or make you feel Good say NO, trust me even if they are hurt, they will eventually recover from it. I lived a lot of my years people pleasing, I made other people happy at my expense, I put other people first, I will agree to commitments even when it was not convenient for me, I will let people have their way even when it is working against me, I will accept lower than my charge for work because I felt I was privileged the person was patronising me, I will let intimidation and disrespectful acts towards me pass because I didn't want to hurt the feelings of someone who didn't care he or she was hurting mine, I spent my time helping other people build their dreams forgetting I had dreams too. All this set the tone for my relationship with friends and family over the years, when I began to love myself, I began to set boundaries and standards, some did not accommodate some friendships I had so I moved on from those associations, I was seen as being selfish at first because I had changed, now that I was focused on building me and not living my life at the expense of others I started losing friends and associates and honestly I was happy about it , because I needed to build friendships that were based on mutual respect. I had established the fact that I mattered and I wasn't going to be tossed around working on other people's dreams because it was time to focus on my dreams and set a standard for how I should be treated. I lost so many "friends" in the process because I stopped running at every call to be at their service or spend valuable time on frivolities keeping their company just to make them happy. At this point my life became productive and I was unapologetic about it.

Be fair to yourself, do not treat yourself like trash, you matter, you matter so much, you are Diamond, you are precious, no one is better than you regardless of status or possession except you tell yourself that, get to work on yourself nothing is more important, live the life you are destined to live, do what makes you happy regardless of what anyone thinks, don't be stuck in a circle seeking the approval of other people , you do not need it , all you need is your approval, you are enough, trust your instincts , believe in yourself. Love yourself, love your own eyes, your own shape, your own style, your own hair, your own car, job, talent, partner, family, and complexion, learn to accept yourself, be enough, be more than enough, when you look in the mirror love who you see completely and totally, don't be under pressure to live up to people's expectation or standards, accept yourself and love yourself and life will begin to feel and be absolutely beautiful.

When you have learnt to love yourself, you will begin to love others the right way, and also make yourself loveable. Most people keep searching for love , they problem is not that you are unlucky with finding love or you have been cursed, the problem is you haven't learnt to love yourself enough to make yourself loveable, take a look at yourself in the mirror and ask yourself honestly can you love the 'YOU' you are looking at right now if you were someone else, would you love a person who nags, has mood swings, has no job, no life goals, no ambition, is very unkempt, depressed, hurt, bitter, resentful, hypocritical , has a foul attitude towards others, judges other people every chance he or she gets, drinks excessively ,smokes heavily and has no life direction , would you love that person? I am thinking your answer is no, so get working on yourself, love yourself enough to make yourself the type of person you would be able to fall in love with. If you truly love yourself you will take care of yourself, you will be honest with yourself, you would not abuse your body, and instead you will build up yourself and make yourself a person of value, who would not love such a person? It is not about the designers you wear, or the makeup, flashy cars and jewelleries you own, it's about being the best you, the you that you can fall in love with, that is the you everyone will come to respect and love. Self-love is being mindful of what you feed yourself, because in the end your life is shaped by it.

CHAPTER
5

WHEN YOU DREAM, ACT

"All you need is an idea, a dream and the will to execute it" … Success Manifest

Your dreams are only mere fantasies until you start acting on them. I am one hell of a dreamer, I could lie in bed and day dream for hours about different versions of my life's successful outcome, get amazing ideas, play them from start to finish in my mind, I have achieved so much and created so much in my life but guess what most of them have only happened in my mind, I would say I just kept fantasizing about them happening but I barely acted on these dreams. That is not even the worst part, most times after a while I see someone else make that dream happen and I say to myself, ah! I thought about this idea a long time ago, yes you did Joy! But you did nothing about it shame on you.

Until we add actions to our dreams they are just mere fantasies, your dreams are God's way of giving your life meaning, it's the reason you wake up with enthusiasm every morning, because you are looking forward to making something happen. The distance between your dreams and reality is action. Have a vision and mission, a life without purpose is a frustrated, unhappy, unfulfilled and wasted life.

You need to believe in that dream whatever it is, even if you think it's ridiculous and almost impossible, believe in your dream enough to take baby steps towards achieving it, all it takes is one foot ahead of the other, little actions every day, doesn't matter how small, as long as you are taking action towards making it happen, take full ownership of your ship, apply yourself every day, open your mind to learning new things, getting better at things that can make you achieve your dreams, whatever it takes keep going . People might laugh at you dream or idea, they will tell you it's impossible, it cannot be done, listen you cannot expect everyone to believe in your dream, it's your dream not theirs, don't let them talk you out of it, just follow through with it. One day they will wake up and the world is a better place thanks to your brave act of making that dream a reality. The world will thank you for adding more beauty and meaning to it. Allow your actions and results speak your truth. Do not limit yourself, you can go as far as your mind can conceive and you let yourself implement. Dare to dream big, don't play small. Push yourself beyond your limits, beyond your comfort zone. I met a young lady who told me she makes clothes for children, she went into mass production and her brand name is Kulture smiths, I didn't understand the magnitude of her work until I saw her work and listened to where she was coming from, she had in six months produced about a 1000 dresses for little girls from her factory in her living room, she was scared when she started but she believed in her dream and started taking it a step at a time, she will buy her fabrics intermittently in small quantities and come up with designs, then her tailors will make them under her supervision, she said sometimes she will wake up and would be blank, no single shred of creativity in her mind, she will then ask God for help and suddenly the concepts for her designs will start popping up in her head, seeing her designs blew me away , they were unique and amazing , you would think those dressing came from big brands abroad because of the neat finishing and beautiful designs, you could tell a lot of hard work, dedication, detail, and focus had been put into her work , I was inspired by her story because many of us are scared of pushing beyond our comfort zone, we are not pushing beyond our limits or applying ourselves to go beyond the ordinary, the easily doable to do extraordinary things. You need to believe in yourself, dream so big it scares you then act on it and make it happen.

Everything you see around you in the world today was created by someone who isn't smarter than you, some people do not even have the opportunities you have today, they just believed in their dream and took action, find your own opportunity and take action, they say success happens when opportunity meets preparation, when you begin to take action the opportunity will present itself. Be resourceful, be diligent, be curious, be a sucker for information, read books, study other people's lives, read their biographies you might learn a thing or two.

Know this, just because you dream it, life doesn't just hand it to you, you must desire what you want, you must want it bad enough to wake up every morning and go to bed every night consumed with the desire to see your dream come to life, you can't just wake up in the morning and say life give it to me you must bring something to the table and that something is called Action. You have to act on your dreams only then can life deliver what is yours to you. You must put in the work, think, use your brain, task your mind to find a way to re-invent yourself and achieve your dreams, I was in an Uber ride and the Uber driver found a very smart way to engage me in a conversation about the Uber business, in less than two minutes he was talking about all the business he does and was subliminally marketing me, I understood what he was doing and I was so thrilled by how driven he was to succeed and the methods he applied in marketing his business, he knew that the days he drove Uber the only way he could market his business was to his passenger , because every passenger he picked up was a potential client, so in the most respectful way he marketed his cassava flakes business to me and told me he had some in his boot and he sold to his passengers, gave me the numbers how much he makes each month selling his Cassava flakes alongside his Uber rides, I was amazed, what intrigued me the most is how he thinks ahead of his potential client , he knew I would probably say I don't eat Cassava flakes so he quickly told me how even the clients who don't eat cassava flakes bought just to encourage him, I smiled to myself, he is a smart guy , when I got to my destination I paid for my trip and bought a pack of cassava flakes even though I wasn't going to eat it , I bought it to encourage him and because I learnt a few things about building my dreams from him, believe it or not , he added some value to me on that trip and the extra cash I spent was worth it.

Getting out of the car, I thought to myself how much one can achieve if only we applied ourselves just a little more like this guy, he definitely has a dream, he is passionate and driven about it and he is taking steps every day to make those dreams a reality, one thing he is doing is thinking outside the box and it is working perfectly well for him, he is one of many Uber drivers but his attitude towards his dream and his desire to succeed has made him stand out, I can bet my money on it that five years down the line he won't be driving an Uber anymore but someone of his colleagues will. The actions you take towards achieving your dreams is what will make you stand out of the crowd. I was reading Oprah's biography and found out that despite the fact that she came from a lowly background and grew up at a time when being black was a disadvantage, she had big dreams, acted on those dreams regardless of how impossible people told her it will be and today she is one of the most famous and successful female entrepreneurs of our time, she fought against all odds and pushed her way to the limelight, today she is one of the most celebrated black women in history.

One of the gravest mistakes we make today, is expecting God to perform magic, we pray day in day out for the realisation of our dreams but do nothing about it, because we have the misconception that once we have prayed, we leave it to God to do the Abracadabra, sorry it doesn't work that way. The problem is we expect God to do what God expects us to do, so the job remains undone and sadly so many dreams go to the grave unrealised, that is why they say the cemetery is where you find the greatest number of untapped talents and unrealised dreams. Dream big, set goals and take massive action. You are solely responsible for your dream materialising, God has done his part he gave you a dream and everything you need to make that dream happen He has put inside of you all that is left is for you to act, it's for you to start taking action towards making that dream a reality, it doesn't matter if its baby steps as long as you are taking action every single day towards the realisation of your dream.

If you do not act on your dreams, someone else will use you to build theirs, take it from someone who has worked with other people on their own dreams for so long, people see the strength and potential you possess, once you do not put them to good use, they will use your strength and potential for their own benefit, at some point you will look back and see that you have wasted your best years building other people's dreams, don't be bitter or mad at them, no one used you , you were responsible for all of it , don't blame anyone, instead push yourself to start working on your dreams now.

Stop making excuses and act on your dreams, stop waiting for enough money, enough courage, enough education or enough cars, stop waiting till you graduate, get married, add weight, lose weight, get fit, or move house, start now, all you need to make you dream happen God has deposited inside of you. I have waited for so many years to act on my dreams because of some of these reasons, time just kept passing by, my best years were slipping away and in all my waiting I discovered that all I needed to put my dreams to work I already had inside of me I was just wasting precious time, I took a decision to start working on my dreams with what I had at my disposal, my mind, gifts, potentials, creative ability and every other thing started falling in place after I took action. You have all you need to succeed inside of you, find it and get to work.

CHAPTER
6

YOU THINK YOU' VE GOT TIME

"If we wait until we are ready, we will be waiting the rest of our lives" Unknown

Don't leave what you can do today for tomorrow, procrastination is the greatest enemy of success. Stop pushing what you can do today to tomorrow, today is a gift don't waste it, make the very best out of it. The greatest lie we tell ourselves is that we have time, life is indeed very short, you don't have all the time in the world, what you have is today, make every second of the day count. Time wasted can never be gotten back, you cannot get this moment which just passed back anymore, that's why we must make very second count.

When you procrastinate you waste your life, time is such a precious gift once it passes you can't get it back. Have you ever put off paying a bill and it kept accumulating until eventually the day comes that you can't put it off again? Did you put off servicing your car tomorrow after tomorrow and eventually your engine knocked or the car developed more problems? How did you feel? Did you like the pressure you were under? Did you have regrets?

Regrets and procrastination go hand in hand because when you procrastinate, you are bound to lose and when you lose regrets follow naturally and you start wishing you had done things differently. Let me share a story with you, my dog had 7 puppies a while back, it was her first litter in two years, I was so excited and I saw it as a source of income, given the breed she is , her puppies are pricy, as they started growing they were so beautiful we chose male and female pups we were going to keep and sold what was left, my vet told me on one of his house visits they were due for vaccination and I said tomorrow, I kept saying tomorrow every day until one day one of the puppies stopped eating , she became withdrawn, we didn't know what was wrong with her so we tried home remedies, we even concluded she was depressed because her brother was sold a day earlier, eventually she started stooling bloody stool with a foul smell then I called the vet, we were told it could be the dreaded parvo virus and they should all be taken to the doctor, by morning she died and all the other 4 puppies were sick, we rushed them to the hospital and they started treated them for parvo, the second female died and we were left with

3 puppies, we were all so sad , in the end the other 3 survived but guess what! Vaccinations would have cost me 18000 naira, I ended up spending over 60000 naira treating them and still lost two puppies because I kept procrastinating. I was full of regrets and promised myself it will never happen again, peaches their mum has littered again and trust me I'm not taking chance with these puppies this time, lesson learnt.

Now this is just about dogs, we play around with even more serious issues in our lives, I can tell you a million stories about my lackadaisical attitude towards my own life. I almost lost my life two years ago because I kept putting off going to the hospital, it was a very close shave with death, and people close to me who knew the story, knew God loved me way too much because the day I finally walked into the hospital I was rushed into the theatre because I was bleeding om the inside and death was minutes away, I was working around for weeks with half a litre of blood leaking out of my body, ignoring all the symptoms and pain and putting off my visit to the doctor everyday but for Gods intervention. Most of us are playing with our lives and destiny just the same way, putting off what we can do today for tomorrow until it takes away a large chunk of us. I have put of so many projects and dreams I should have gotten done years and years ago in life, because I procrastinated or listen to someone who told me it was a waste of time or it wouldn't work or because I was afraid, I might fail, most of all I was waiting for the right time. Never allow waiting to become a habit, live your dreams in the moment, life is happening now.

I have learnt to do what I can in the moment, take advantage of every minute and every day, make it count, live everyday like it's your last, because you never know what tomorrow might bring. The moment you realise how important time is your entire perspective will change, think about it, what are the things you wouldn't leave undone if today was your last day on earth? yes I see you making a list, now take that list and get to work, it's time to make your life count, don't be a waste, don't let God second guess His creation, He never makes mistakes. You are here for a reason, find that reason and make it count, if you have found it, get to work regardless of your shortcomings or challenges, if you die today what are the dreams that will die with you , business that will never be set up, books that will never be written, songs that will never be sang, talents that will never be put to use, buildings that will never be built, companies that will be never established, that agent of change the world is waiting for will never be born, lives that will never be touched, Nations that will never be healed or liberated because you never took action. This is a wakeup call, Make NOW a favourite word, make that phone call now, call that meeting now, start that book now, start that project now, go into that studio now, propose to that lady now, service that car now, fix that roof now, DO IT NOW.

CHAPTER
7

PROTECT YOUR ENERGY

"Flowers need to be nurtured, watered, given sunlight, protected and loved. Why would you allow anyone who isn't about that in your garden?" Unknown

Everything around you are made up of energy, give out what you want to get back, energy is contagious either you affect people or you infect people, your energy flows where your attention goes, you draw to yourself the people and events that resonate with the energy you are radiating, you attract what you are, it is important to pay attention to who your energy increases or decreases around, that is a hint on who you should keep close or who you should stay away from. There are certain things that drain your energy you must make a conscious effort to stay away from them, things like holding on to the past, worrying unnecessarily, over thinking, complaining all the time, gossiping, people pleasing, condoning toxic associations will not only drain your energy but alter it as well. There is always a message in the way a person treats you, just listen, listen to what they are not saying, watch their actions and feel their energy.

Be too busy becoming the best version of yourself that you don't have the time and energy to involve yourself with negativity, drama, the past or things that drain you. Be defined by what you do not what others have done to you, don't give people that kind of power over you. The better you become the better you attract, every moment you have a choice to use your energy to be productive or to let the behaviour of others control your flow of energy. Stop letting others weigh you down, stop overthinking or over processing everything, learn to let go of what you cannot control. Start taking care of your mind by thinking more positive optimistic thoughts, take care of your body so you can be healthy and feel good, take care of your soul by filing it with love and laughter, this will guarantee success in every area of your life. When you learn to control your reaction to situations and people around you take back your power and protect your energy.

Beware of toxic people they come with a lot drama, drama that will drain your energy and keep you stagnant and disoriented. I have great news for you , no one bothers a nobody , greatness attracts a lot of critics as much as it attracts a lot of friends, some mean well, others are just out to crush you and see that you never get anywhere in life, then there is that interesting group they are not your critics neither are they your enemies , they just don't love themselves or feel good about themselves so when they talk to people they speak nothing but vile words, their words are venomous meant to break your spirit, they cannot tell you anything positive or encouraging even if they wanted to, they will never applaud you , these set of people only see the faults in everything even where you can't find faults they are trained in the art .

The moment they see you, they start condemning everything you do, say , wear, plan to do , everything is red to them, now that's not the worse part , they are an authority on everything including your life. This set of people you never should entertain, never take their words seriously, it is not about you it's about them. People can only meet you as deeply as they have met themselves, when people say mean things to you it is because they don't know better, it reveals their unhealed parts, it's a reflection of how they feel inside and you should not take it personal or get mad, just pray for them.

I will tell you a story about a family friend of ours, he could be very generous to you financially or materially but each time you are in his presence you don't leave filled even if you came filled you leave drained and empty, because he sucks the joy and life out of you with his words, his words are venomous, when you tell him about your dreams and goals, he belittles them and talks you down, people tolerated it but I knew that it was wrong on so many levels. One day I was having a conversation with him and he said some very mean words to me about things I held dear in my life, then it hit me, it's not about me, it was about him and his unhealed parts, at that point I felt compassion for him, because if only he knew better, he will be better, I knew he was in a place where all he felt was what he was giving out. Thinking about my conversation with him for a few days I began to see a pattern, he always says mean stuff not just to me but anyone who he had the opportunity to roast. He talks down to people for no reason, I for one knew I did not deserve to be treated that way by anyone, no one deserves to be treated that way, I knew I was better than that, I blamed myself for condoning such toxicity for so long so I made up my mind to cut off from him not because I was mad but because I loved myself too much to keep relating with someone who kills my spirit, discourages me and saps my energy every chance he gets.

What you feed your mind is very important, that is the breeding ground for everything you will ever be, manifest or create, that means you need to be careful what you hear, let yourself see, take in or think about, there is so much garbage going on around us every day, what you give ear to or pay attention to can make or destroy you. I stopped relating with that man because if I kept going, I will turn my mind into a garden of resentfulness and bitterness, this means I become too angry to be productive, because his vile words will begin to take root in my mind, subliminally creeping in and controlling my thoughts and action and I might even begin to believe his words and start second guessing myself. Who we let into our lives matter a whole lot, it's important to protect your energy, in protecting it you are protecting your life? When you let situations or people control how you feel, you give them the power to control your life, how you feel creates the climate for what you become and what you emit. To protect your energy, it is ok to cancel that appointment, not answer that call, spend time alone, walk away, take the day off, say what you feel regardless of whose ox is god, burn that bridge, whatever it takes to keep your energy right do it. When you wake up in the morning, own your energy, fix yourself from the inside, make up your mind to stay happy, positive and proactive the whole day regardless of whatever is ahead of you, no matter what is meant to provoke you or bring you down, choose to live above it, just keep your head up and stay positive, don't give in to negative feelings. You want to be successful, fulfilled and happy then watch what you let in because it determines what you bring out.

CHAPTER
8

KNOW YOUR POISON

If you know what weakens you, admit it to yourself, accept it and stay very far from it. We all have weaknesses, coming to terms with them helps us find the strength in it. You must identify them first then apply its antidote.

I discovered anger had a great hold on me, when I lose it I make so many mistakes, especially with my words and actions and I regret them most times, now anger was just the beginning, when it became comfortable living inside me it invited its friend's un-forgiveness and bitterness. I had to deal with this demons and poisons for years. When I am angry with a person I can go on for years holding on to the hurt and grudge, when I think about the person my tummy will twist and turn , my heart will bleed, I will be so mad, I will re-affirm my position not to forgive or forget , if I had to speak about or to the person, you could taste the bitterness from my speech, it was horrible but that wasn't the worst part , the worst part was what it was doing to me , it was ruining my life, the venom I was brewing was not hurting the person it was destroying me.

The devil is so crafty, he knows how to use your poison or your weakness to ruin your life or keep you from achieving your God given destiny. My name is joy, it is a powerful name and this name was the foundation on which my life was built. I am a very joyful person, it resonates from the very depth of me, not to blow my own trumpet but I have been told my smile is so infectious, I enter a room with my face lit with a smile every time, you cannot stay sad or have a dull moment around me, I am an empath by nature I can feel peoples pain and connect with the emotions they are feeling, I get broken and shed tears at the site of the suffering of others, now when God deposits all this beautiful qualities in a person , the devil has a way of working his own magic to keep you from using all these beauty inside you to touch your world, so he starts to feed on your weaknesses , so like poison they start taking over your mind and life if you let them, you cannot imagine how destructive it can get.

When you are angry, bitter and resentful, it destroys you not the person you have those feelings towards. On the other hand, letting go of these negative emotions are not easy at all, sometimes you want to but you don't know how. You need God's help and a conscious decision to loosen your grip on whatever it is. Your strengths and weakness are all part of your whole make up, everyone comes with them, but which ever you focus on helps to supress the presence and effect of the other.

I was very angry and bitter at my son's father for years, I didn't know it was responsible for a few setbacks I experienced in the first few years after I had my son, until God started speaking to me on forgiveness and teaching me to let go and love unconditionally. He made me understand bitterness and anger had taken root in my heart and because they were negative emotions nothing positive can grow there, I fought it at first because I felt I had every right to feel the way and felt, God told me I did but He also told me those feelings were destroying me and I had to let them go. I couldn't create anything positive and beautiful in my mind even if I wanted to because it wouldn't live long enough to manifest because the weeds and poisons of anger, bitterness and unforgiveness will kill them. Every positive emotion that could have propelled my growth and success were suffocating because I was embracing too much negativity. When God open my eyes to this home truth, I surrendered to his healing power, made peace with my past and moved on with my life, today I can't begin to tell you the transformation I have experienced ever since. Letting go of those feeling doesn't mean you got an apology or the problem was fixed, it means you decided to fix yourself, fix your life and that's what is most important.

Whatever you cannot control let it go, don't let it control you, you can't control people's actions towards you but you can control how you react to them and how you let them affect you. I read somewhere that if it wouldn't matter in five years, do not spend five minutes on it and that is one of my mantras. Bitterness and anger are like cancers they eat so deep inside you, they destroy everything, physically, emotionally, psychologically. You must find a way to channel all that energy, for me when am angry I quickly focus on the good, sometimes it's hard to think about the good things a person has done when you are so mad at them, but if you just focus on the good you will find some more, when you find them be grateful for them and you will feel the angry emotions melting away, this means the anger does not last long enough for its goons' bitterness, resentment and the lot to take root. Once you reject that first negative emotion, every other negative emotion that resonates from it goes away.

What is your poison, whatever it is, ask yourself is it worth losing everything? Is it worth losing your life? Yours might not be innate, it might be an addiction that is holding you back, drugs, alcohol, violence, sowing wild oats, or maybe you are verbally abusive, whatever it is one thing we are sure of is you are better off without it but the choice is yours. You need to recognise and even accept you have a problem first and foremost, own it then and only then can you live above it, a lot of people live in denial about their weakness, they refuse to admit it, some actually know but prefer to masquerade it, in the end accepting who you are in totality both the good and the bad helps you rise above your weaknesses.

Everything you do is conceived in the mind, whatever you become is first conceived in your mind, if you let negativity and evil take root in your mind, you can hardly be productive. Know your poison, your weakness and find its antidote, something positive and productive, channel your energy towards it, it is a choice, you have to make a choice to choose the high road and not let negativity control you , when you make that choice, believe it or not you have saved your precious life.

CHAPTER
9

THE COMPANY YOU KEEP

*"Everyone in a ship with Jonah experienced a storm
because of his disobedience to God"*
*"When setting out on a journey do not seek advice
from those who never left home"*

The people you spend your time with and the people you give your attention determines how far you will go in life. Who you connect to will determine the outcome of your life. A great man once said "show me five people you call friends and I will tell you where you will be in five years". Stop and take a poll of your close friends then evaluate where you are in life and where they are, do you think you are in good company? When you have three friends who are always broke, believe me you will make the fourth one. You attract what you associate with, even though am not a fan of the phrase fake it until you make it, I am a believer in positioning yourself for the future or life you want. If you want to be a successful entrepreneur in the future begin to act like one now, make friends with people that will inspire you and stir you towards your dream, find mentors who can propel you towards that future, read books, attend events and seminars, engage in activities that will prepare you for the life you want, dress the part, talk the part most of all choose your friends wisely. You cannot desire success and keep the company of loafers or idle mind, that desire will probably never become a reality because your association makes it impossible for you to work towards your goal.

Time is a very precious commodity, when you waste it you can never get it back, time tip toes by so fast you barely know how much time you have wasted until it is gone. Some friends are time wasters, my pastor says the worst thing that can happen to a person is associating with people going in a different direction, when people are not going the same direction with you, they will waste your time, it means you have no business keeping the company of people who are not on the same journey as you, you will definitely miss your flight. When you sit with them all you do is engage in idle talk or indulge in unproductive activities, by the time you know it the whole day is gone and you achieve absolutely nothing. When people do not respect you time, it is not because they are mean or selfish, it because you did not draw boundaries by showing them how much you value your time, when you make yourself excessively available for other people's comfort or at their disposal, they will disrespect your time because you have made it excessively available to them. I had a client once who got really fond of me, I came to see her as an aunt of some sort, whenever I went for a consultation with her and I have spare time I would help her out with stuff at home, after a while it wasn't about me helping anymore, she will demand I do stuff for her, sometimes she will call from work and ask that I go over to her place to help out, forgetting I should be working too , with time it became a norm, whenever I had an appointment with her , that day I don't get to do anything else except her work. There are days I will head home by almost 12midnight , one day I was driving out of her gate and I told myself this is absolutely wrong on so many levels, this is an abuse of my time and no amount of love or fondness should make someone abuse another person's time this way, but guess what it wasn't her fault I was the one who devalued my time not her, she only treated my time the way I showed her, so I made up my mind to right that wrong .I stopped showing up when I know it's not official and when I know I don't have the time, she was offended at first and stopped reaching out to me , months later she reached out to me because she had a job for me, she told me she wasn't happy I was hardly coming around, and I explained to how busy I was and how much sacrifice it was taking to make those visits, she understood and we made up, now when she calls me for a favour she wants to first make sure I am free and it was convenient for me , she began to value my time because I established those boundaries, now we are back in business but only this time , my time is respected.

The people you associate with affects your life on so many levels both physically and spiritually. When you yoke yourself with someone who is walking the wrong path you will deal with the consequences as well. When you associate with the wrong crowd there is always a high price to pay in the end. I have had some wrong association growing up and it set me back a handful of years and I had to deal with the consequences of my choices. The wrong association can destroy your reputation and integrity, these are two things that takes a lot to build, very little to destroy and a whole lot more to build back.

Who are you looking up to? Some people are not meant to be your mentors because they will mislead you, chose your mentors wisely don't choose mentors because of their "packaging", mentorship goes beyond that, mentorship is about the innate substance, the quality of knowledge and wisdom your mentor possesses that you have the privilege to drink from. Most times you have no business looking up to the people you are looking up to, you are confiding in people you have no business confiding in, if you just believed in yourself a little more, you will find out you have more to give them than they could ever give you, you have more substance inside of you. You have to know who you are, know what you have inside of you, don't be intimidated by what you see on the outside, they real deal is on the inside, most people mask the emptiness on the inside with so much aggression, big English, swag, intimidation, or even affluence so you don't see what is underneath. Sometimes some people feel the need to crush you and put you down every chance they get, the truth is they need you to stay down, it makes them feel better about themselves and it makes them feel superior, and makes you feel the need to look up to them, I read something written by Tera Carissa Hodges that sometimes people try to destroy you, precisely because they recognise your power, they see it and do not want it to exist. Do not look up to someone who has nothing to offer you, ask God for the spirit of discernment so you can recognise the real deal when you see it.

The company you keep should be determined by the value a person adds to your life, do they leave you empty or full? Do they drain you or nourish you? Are your values and goals in sync? You have to be sure your soul is being fed right, what you let in is responsible for what you become. I have a wonderful friend each time I visit her, I leave her presence blessed and full, I always leave with something valuable for my business, my life or my relationship with people, her conversations with me are always progressive and a blessing to me, I always look forward to visiting her because she is truly a blessing. When you spent time with a person and you always leave their presence drained you need to reduce to the barest minimum your association with such a person, because you are growing weeds that will kill your flowers with such association. You need to apply wisdom in your associations, know that the company you keep and the people you associate with goes a long way to define you, there is a popular saying "show me your friends and I will tell you who you are" and "birds of the same feathers flock together", a lot of people have been grossly misunderstood because of the company they kept in the past or are keeping, you might feel because you do not partake in most of their vices you are different , dear friend sorry to break it to you , you will not be in the long run, it is only a matter of time before they start indulging you and you start off with little compromises, then eventually the big ones, it is easier to pull some one down the ladder than for that person to pull you up, as a young girl I made some bad calls in friendships and I am a fast learner , I have the ability to be better than my teacher, so you can imagine how many bad calls I made growing up but for God's grace and mercy, the Bible says bad company corrupts good morals, be wise!

The smaller your circle the simpler your life, associate with people who share the same values and life goals with you, iron sharpens iron, it is easier to understand each other and encourage each other to grow.

CHAPTER
10

IF YOU STUMBLED MAKE IT PART OF THE DANCE

"Don't be afraid to fail, be afraid to try" Unknown

I read a book years ago titled failing forward by John Maxwell, it was an amazing book, the book embodies the side of failing people hardly look at, this is the part that failing is a part of success, when you fail don't give up don't see it as the end of the world, it means you tried and that means you have learned something so you are armed to try again. Success comes with failing so many times without giving up. If the Wright brothers had given up on trying over and over again at perfecting the airplane, we won't have them today or Thomas Edison on the light bulb, we probably will still be using lanterns, I don't think any inventor got it right the first try, I don't think Microsoft or Apple got it right the first time, they kept on trying and trying , with each year bringing a new modification and upgrade to the last, today we see what happens when you do not give up, we see that failing is not the end of the story.

In life some of you will dabble into some many things just like me, try out one brilliant idea after another and meet deadlocks, people will even give up on you, they will stop believing in your ability to succeed, don't give up, in fact that is a reason to prove them wrong, keep going, the only thing you need, is you believing in yourself, as long as you believe in you that is all you need. I have tried so many businesses and projects in the past, a lot of then have failed along the line, one thing was constant I learnt a different priceless lesson each time, lessons I wouldn't have learnt from business school. On the other hand, I can also assure you that a lot of people had given up on me making it happen, that didn't stop me, today the story is different because I didn't give up.

Learn from your failures, the secret to your success is hidden in why you failed, so don't give up, find it, apply it and try again, when you stumble make it part of the dance, just keep going. Most times when we fail, we become too ashamed or afraid to go on, because people laughed at us, talked us down and so on, you can't let all that keep you down, you need to get right back up and make it happen.

I have started so many projects in my life I abandoned along the way because I failed at some point or the other, or I got turn down at some point or the other, today I see people who persevered in the same field and have recorded huge successes. The difference between failure and success is your perspective and mind set, do you see your failure as a temporary setback or a permanent fall. I have learnt to go back to the drawing board whenever I fail and find a new way to succeed, I have also learnt to be deaf to my audience booing and focus on the goal I want to achieve, trust me I have been mocked and laughed at so many times but that hasn't stopped me.

For 9 years I have had a dream of having a talk show, I have tried so many times to get it going but I have always had challenges in getting it started, while my dream was still incubating , my sister started her own talk show, which has been a huge success, one day I was on her set and a member of her production team who I was talking to a while back about getting mine started, looked at me and said "you have been talking about starting a talk show long before your sister, what's going on see how far she has gone , we still haven't seen anything from you" he had a smirk on his face , as if he was mocking me , my sister looked at me because she knows me so well and knows how sensitive I am , but I guess she must have been surprised at my reply , I just said time and chance happens to us all and I smiled and moved on. Unknown to him I was already working on my talk show, I just hadn't mentioned it to any one yet.

I wasn't about to let his mocking me discourage me or weigh me down or make me blab out what I was cooking in silence. I know the challenges I have had to go through with that same project, challenges that have grown me to a point where I understand the role time plays in birthing our dreams if I didn't know any better, I would have given up on the dream of having that talk show but I kept pushing, I was in the labour room pushing and I wasn't about to let anyone distract me from getting my baby out. I did not know when that dream will be a reality but all I know is I was not giving up on it.

Stay focused on your goal, no matter how many times you fall get up and keep going. You failed an exam, write it again, you added weight after losing it, lose it again, just don't give up. My weight loss journey has been one of the most challenging episodes in my life. I love food, and I binge a lot, plus I do a lot of comfort eating, welcome to my world, I tried all the fad diets and weight loss drinks and pills, I lose the weight and get back on again, I was like a yoyo, you see me this month am slim, you see me next month I have put it all back on. I sat down and decided to understand what I was doing wrong that was making me fail, I discovered it was the short cuts and crash diets, so I decided to do it right this time, exercise and eat right, of course it worked for a longer period of time but then I relapsed again and again. I didn't give up, I went back to my drawing board to understand what the problem was, and I discovered it was lack of discipline. I had the right formula for weight loss, I was even paid by clients to help them lose weight, but I had no discipline with food and exercise, I knew what to eat but I ate at the wrong times sometimes, I fell of the wagon too often, I would lazily stay away from exercising and procrastinate because I was tired or didn't want to miss my favourite soap opera or couldn't just get out of bed on time, in no time I will pile on the pounds again. Finding out why I was failing was my problem half solve, next step was applying myself, being disciplined and holding myself accountable, I am still a work in progress but looking back, where am now is better than where I am coming from, and am proud of my progress, success is an ongoing process, every day I get through without a wrong meal or with a little work out is progress for me and I celebrate it, no matter how little every time you achieve a landmark victory that is success and you must acknowledge it, celebrate it and keep going.

Failures show us what we need to do better. Coca cola sold 25 bottles of Coke their first year, they didn't pack up and give up on the brand, today Coca cola is the leading soda brand in the world, raking in billions of dollars every year. Most times we focus too much on failing itself we miss the lesson in it, the lesson that is supposed to make our work better. No matter how many times you fail do not give up, keep trying over and over again until you get it right, the good news is each time you try again as you open yourself to learn and figure out what made you fail, you improve your mastery and eventually you will get it right, if you don't fail you will never learn, if you don't learn you will never change or come into full realisation of your full potential and what you are built to accomplish. It is very important to learn to live above the noise, people will point out your failures to you every time, there will be a lot of side talks and talk downs, people will try to compare your growth to other people's success, do not be moved, you will have your turn on the stage of life as long as you keep working towards it undaunted and unshaken by the noise.

The road to success is a tough one, but it is achievable, you will get doors closed against you, you will get so many Nos but do not give up, most times no is a yes that needs a little persuasion, giving up is not an option. You can start late, stumble, fall down, make mistakes, be mocked, be ridiculed, be laughed at, whatever you do just make sure you keep going and reach the finish line.

CHAPTER
11

SAME LIGHTS DIFFERENT LAMPS

"There is in each of us so much goodness that if we could see its glow it would light up the world"

One of the greatest injustices you can do to yourself is looking down on yourself and thinking someone else is better than you. Most times it's not our faults, it's the abuse we have to deal with from parents, partners and our immediate environment. If you are a parent who is fond of comparing your children to other people's children, expecting them to behave like other children, you need to stop it NOW, if you are a partner who compares your spouse to other people you need to stop it. When you grow up with low self-esteem you tend to feel you are not good enough, you lack the confidence to stand with your peers, when you live with being talk down to or compared to other people long enough it goes a long way to keep you from ever knowing what you are made of or capable of.

I am going to tell you a secret, there is nothing you lack, you are blessed with gifts and potentials inside you, some you are even yet to discover because your environment and your mind is limiting you and has not allowed you explore yourself completely. If you watch any of the super hero movies, I love them because they message they send is amazing especially for our kids, you always see a regular boy or girl who is probably bullied and outsized by his peers and treated like nobody, how he is treated makes him look inside most times drawing from the rage, pain, desperation to save, or determination to be better which ever it is , pushes himself harder beyond his ordinary ability and then he discovers that he is no ordinary or insignificant person like he has been made to believe , but a hero with special powers to save the world .

We are all Heroes with special powers, born for the sole purpose of saving our world, we all just have different powers, like the x-men we have different abilities that make us special, just that some powers are visible to see and others are innate and it takes extra effort to see or know they are there, while some people are music maestros, Screen gods or inspirational orators others might be blessed with the gift to feel the pain of others and help them heal, that is why no one should compare you to anyone, and you too should not compare yourself to anyone, you are unique and special in your own way. God has deposited potentials in every one of us and every gift or potential is just as important as the other, the problem is some of us want to be like other people, we want the gift another possesses because of all the razzmatazz around the people, we are so smitten we forget to look inside and discover what we have inside, when you lose your originality you lose your essence, you might never grow into your true self, except you begin to look inward and cultivate your own God given gifts.

Your passion is your driving force, what are you passionate about? I Love movies, I love to talk philosophy, history and life's essence, I love learning about cultures and new things, if I travelled to a foreign country, I will probably go check out historical sites instead of shopping, don't get me wrong I love shopping too, I love dancing, writing, cooking, I love reading books, I could go on and on, all these interests play major roles in who am growing into. The things I am passionate about are totally different from what some other person will be passionate about, staying true to the passion is the only way I can be fulfilled in life. Passion validates purpose as DNA validates paternity.

Your calling is always tied to what you are passionate about, if you are feeling lost and confused about what you should be doing with your life, ask yourself what you are passionate about, your calling is definitely in there somewhere. I have a dear friend who is so passionate about dance, he is a geologist by training but he loves to dance, he dances everywhere without knowing he is dancing, he moves even when he sleeps it's incredible, he is so passionate about it he took it up as a profession and career, even when he didn't know what he was meant to do with it. Later in life it hit him when people started sending him messages and telling him how he has touched their lives with his art in ways he cannot even imagine, some got over their depression, some got some sort of inspiration from his interpretation of his art, some lost weight and experienced tremendous improvement with their health, the list goes on and on. Even when the future was bleak, he stayed true to the art, today he is one of the most successful dancers in the country, because he recognised, he was unique and followed his own passion.

Find your own light, what makes you different is what makes you unique, it is still what makes you standout. A lot of people go through life trying so hard to be someone else, they virtually live in the shadow of another their whole life, this is one of the reasons some people feel so unfulfilled. Dare to be original, you have something the world needs that is why you are here, reach inside and find what that is, find what your calling is, what you super power is and play you role in saving the world. You are here to do something on this earth that only you can do, if you keep trying to live someone else's life your unique soul expression is lost.

CHAPTER
12

BE ORIGINAL

"Dare to be different the world is full of ordinary
"RVM

We all have different unique callings, it's buried in your passion, you know it because it is that one thing that gives you peace, joy and fulfilment when you indulge in it and it's that thing that stirs your soul up. That is what makes you Original and Unique, it is your niche, the part of you that announces you to the world, that thing that expresses your true potential, it is the place you work your magic.

Most times people get carried away wanting other people's life that they waste years of their lives living other people's lives or dreams, funny enough some pull it off and become very successful role playing, but remain unfulfilled and unhappy on the inside, they mask it on the outside but they go through so much suffering on the inside, no amount of success makes them happy, there is always a hunger on the inside they struggle to satisfy, they buy all the most expensive things, take the most exotic holidays, take the most breath-taking partners, buy the biggest houses, still nothing quenches that thirst, this is because the life they live isn't theirs , their purpose and calling still remains untapped and unaccomplished and until they find their way back to who they truly are supposed to be , that peace, joy and fulfilment will continue to evade them.

When you learn to believe in yourself, there is no limit to what you can achieve , you are here on this earth because you have a unique part to play, nobody else can play your role better than you , when you decide to take on someone else's role you leave yours unattended to , you begin to give God a reason why you shouldn't even be here in the first place, a wise man once said when you walk in the foot prints of others you won't make any of your own, don't live in someone else's shadow you will be stuck in the dark . It is the original thinkers, artists and inventors throughout history that have created this world of endless possibilities we live in and experience.

Be yourself the world celebrates originality, there is just one life for each of us, our own and the most important component for being original in this day of copies is a definite dream. The most exhausting thing in life is trying so hard to be what or who you are not or who you are not meant to be.

To be nobody but yourself in a world which is doing its best to make you conform to the crowd means to fight the hardest battle of your existence, once you conform to do what others do going with the crowd you get lost in the crowd. Nobody can be you or better than you can be, that makes you really special, embrace that individuality, you are you no one can be you more than you could ever be. Stay true to who you are and the world will eventually celebrate you.

When you keep living someone else's life, the life you are born to live goes to waste. Be a trendsetter, be a game changer, set the pace, bring on something new, don't plagiarise, create something new, something from within and let the world celebrate you for your originality

CHAPTER

13

DANCE TO YOUR OWN MUSIC

"If a man does not keep pace with his companions perhaps it is because he hears a different drummer. Let him step to the music which he hears, however measured or far away" ... **Henry David Thoreau**

Life is not an Olympics competition, know that you are not in competition with anyone. Your path to greatness or success is charted for you and you alone, just because someone else got there first doesn't make you a failure, just because someone else is being celebrated now, doesn't mean your time to be celebrated won't come.

People have found themselves in trouble and even huge debts because of the need to compete with the success of another. Some have married the wrong spouses in the bid to compete with their friends who got married, they have ended up in hell instead of a marriage. I have heard parents say "I want my child to study medicine like Mr A's son", "I want my daughter to marry a rich man like Mrs B's daughter", some of this pressure parents put on their children out of the desire to compete with other parents or bring out the best in their children have ruined the lives and futures of their children, these children are put under pressure to walk paths they do not want to walk, they are not destined to work or are not ready to walk yet.

When I was in the university, I saw a lot of competition going on between girls on campus, everyone wanted to out shine the other, the competition was over everything from shoes, clothes, jewelleries to boyfriends, to owning a car on campus, the latest mobile phone name it, the competition was on about everything except who came out with a first class, funny isn't it? That would have been some healthy competition, striving to be the best but the sort of competition going on was making young people do unspeakable things just to impress their peers. Imagine when a child from a lowly home is competing with a child from a rich home in the show of affluence, what you get is a child who goes into a life of crime and immorality to measure up.

As adults competition is very much a part of our lives, especially amongst friends and siblings. Never envy another's success, focus on your own path, time and chance happens to us all, focus on you goals, be content with the life you have, be grateful for where you are, believe me there are people who still want the life, spouse, property, job, business, dress, body type, complexion you hate or do not appreciate. Be confident in who you are, do not try to be who you are not just to fit in, dare to stand out, don't be intimidated by other people's possessions, don't make compromises just because you want to fit in or be noticed. Be yourself, be original, be a trendsetter eventually people will come to respect your originality.

Learn to love your life, your path, your pace, own it and just because it happened for someone else now and it hasn't happened for you doesn't mean it won't eventually happen for you. Every flower has its time to bloom, every plant has its own season, every animal had its own gestation period, an elephant births just one elephant once in two years while a dog has up to eight puppies in two months, but guess what, in due season they all deliver their young ones. Maybe your announcement is coming like that of the elephant, after two years, what she drops shakes the earth, when her baby crosses the road cars stop, people stop to marvel at such great wonder, do not envy the arrival of the dogs puppies, yes they look cute, yes they come in numbers, but your time is coming when you eventually birth your elephant the world will notice this remarkable event and celebrate it, because what you carry is no ordinary baby , it is a special, uncommon and unique one, one that comes once in two years. Celebrate the lifting of others because your lifting will surely come, stay on your course your sail will come in , it is the law of nature, as long as you focus and keep working at it. Instead of trying to live someone else's life or competing with others, focus on your goals and dreams, work hard at building them , stay on your lane, most times when we do not have definiteness of purpose we find ourselves running in different directions, once we find out someone was successful in a particular field we decided to run with that tide, when we find out someone else is cashing out in something else we abandon the first one and run with the next tide, you are in the business of everybody's business, you have no purpose, direction or focus, in the long run you will end up frustrated and unfulfilled.

You need to ignore what everyone else is doing and achieving. Your life is about breaking your own limits and outgrowing yourself to live your best life, you are not in competition with anyone else, plan to outdo your past self not other people. Your life is already a miracle of Chance waiting for you to shape its destiny, take what is yours and run with it, fulfil your own destiny, give meaning to your own existence.

CHAPTER
14

MIRROR MIRROR ON THE WALL

"Flaunt the master piece that is you" Toosturkson

It may look like I am repeating myself in this chapter but the truth is it is imperative I share this little lesson, about loving yourself just the way you look physically, loving your physical appearance is very important. For as long as I can remember I have battled with my weight , I have always wanted to be slimmer because I loved how slim ladies looked, I have always wanted to be curvier , back then I loved how they turned heads, I thought I will get a good man and settle down on time if I was a bit slimmer, curvier, had longer hair, a high pitch voice, was less friendly , talked less and all name it, years later I came to the understanding that if I do not love and accept how I look, no one will, and I found out it took more than a slim body, curvy shape and all those things I yearned for to feel fulfilled or settle down , these are not the criteria, besides I was getting it all wrong backwards, I didn't need to become someone else to be loved, I needed to love myself and be with someone who loves me just the way I am.

I simply did not appreciate and love the body God gave me, inside of seeing how tall I am, my beautiful smile, my smooth skin, my beautiful soft brown skin, my presence, my lovely shape, my size that complimented my stature, I just chose to see negativity, not because all these qualities were not there, because I am beautiful and wonderful made, but because I failed to notice and appreciate this master piece God created and I wanted to look like someone else.

The truth is when we see other people looking all perfect, that perfection is your perspective of the person, you will be surprised to know that person doesn't feel that way about his or her self and will give anything to be like you. Beauty they say is in the eye of the beholder that means beauty means different things to different people, my perception of beauty might not be yours. That is why we see a lady with a man or vice versa and we wonder what he or she saw in the other, you can't see what they saw because it's not your perception of beauty. What draws a person to you is primarily how you feel about yourself, once you love yourself and see yourself as desirable, you will attract people to that light you have ignited within you but when you dim your light on the inside because you do not think you are pretty enough, good enough, eloquent enough, smart enough, curvy enough, chiselled enough then people will see you that way.

I am not saying we shouldn't take care of our appearance, on the contrary it is very important we do but first you must love and accept who you are, and if you feel you need to make changes to how you look, they must be for the right reasons. Until I came to terms with the right reason why I wanted to lose weight, I never recorded permanent success, until I gave up the need to have a beach body and wear size 8 dresses like a model for no absolute reason, my weight loss journey was a yoyo story. I will lose it and add it back , because I didn't have a well-grounded reason so I kept falling off the band wagon, until I woke up one day and found out that my weight was threatening my health and if I didn't do something about it I will have serious issues in the future, I took fitness and healthy eating more seriously, I made it a life style and not a quick fix scheme to impress someone or draw attention at an event or whatever reasons we do this things other than to really make a difference inside.

So many times, I hear ladies say, I don't like my arms they are two big, my tummy is too big, I'm guilty of this particular one, my thighs are too big and so on, it drops their self-esteem and confidence because the stay conscious of it, there is a rejection of some part that contributes to the whole of the person and that is where the problem lies. You have to own that part of you, love it and accept it and then work on making it better if there is need be, but do not see it as a short coming or stumbling block from you living your life. Has anyone ever noticed that those things we often complain about, people never see it? In fact, people that really care about you never ever see it and if whatever you are not loving about yourself is truly a problem to you, let's say you are overweight, people who really care about you will love and support you through dealing with it. What I am saying in essence is struggling to be someone else or changing a part of you to suit your audience isn't good for you, it defeats the purpose of people accepting and loving you for who you are when you have to be someone else to be accepted or celebrated. These days people focus so much on the outside and forget the inside, you see people get face surgeries, butt surgeries, hair transplant, liposuctions just to look different and love their bodies, but the more they do these body enhancement procedures the more they feel the need to do more with an endless hunger and insatiable need for more, through all this no work is done on the inside, when you fix the inside you see the outside differently, you will not feel the need to enhance your look on the outside to feel better about yourself. In the end people will see the outside exactly how you see it. Confidence I have come to realise is the greatest outfit anyone can wear, once you are confident about who you are, how you look and you are in no way intimated about other people regardless of how much they can spend on their looks or what they wear, that confidence is what people see on the outside.

When you keep wanting to look like someone else or keep wanting things you do not have you keep postponing your life from happening, no matter what you do you remain unfulfilled, unsatisfied and unhappy. That is why when you get one plastic surgery you want to get a billion more until you ruin your body to a point when you have to be on the botched TV show or when you want lighter skin, you bleach to a point where you smell and ruin your protective skin layer and have terrible sun burns, black patches and red skin so bad that you have to use heavy foundation to conceal and spend a fortune looking for treatment and creams to correct this irreparable damage, that is why you lose weight to a point which you become anorexic, bulimic or grossly underweight, putting your health at risk from trying out different fad diets and weight loss elixirs, I could go on and on.

Just love yourself, accept yourself, know that God didn't make a mistake creating you how he created you. If you must work on yourself, make sure it is needed and it is for the right reasons, if you had wrong eating habits and you have added weight , its ok to lose it , if you had a baby and need to burn off the fat , that's fine too, if your doctor says your health depended on it , that is also fine, make sure your reasons puts your body first , don't treat your body like it's an experimental piece, love it, take care of it , it's the only one you have to live in , You were fearfully and wonderfully made, God doesn't make mistakes, He knew that was the best nose, arms, thighs, face, complexion for you, LOVE IT.

CHAPTER
15

DON'T TAKE IT PERSONAL

" Maturity is learning to walk away from people and situations that threaten your peace of mind, values, self-respect, morals or self-worth." Unknown

Peoples action towards you is only a reflection of them not you, we live in a world where people make it their business to help you run your life, it is a world where people believe that their opinion of your life is law, this a world where people want to judge your reasons, your thoughts, your feelings, your motives, your choices, your life and the list goes on and on.

Know this people are continually going to make it their business to judge you, judge your actions, dictate how you should live your life, criticise your decision, talk you down, discourage you from pursuing your dreams, it is a given, but the problem is not people doing all these, what matters is your reaction to all these, what matters is how you let all of it affect you. You need to learn to live above people's judgement and criticisms. Learn to detect distractions and avoid them, I read a quote somewhere which says "choose your battles wisely" you can't react to every stone thrown at you, you have to learn to discern what deserves your attention and what does not. I used to be a victim of my emotions, I react easily to everything I hear or every criticism, or toxic drama thrown at me, I was easily drawn into it and in the end, I am emotional distraught, taking days, weeks or even months for me to get over whatever the situation was. I used to be easily bothered about people's opinion of me, I lose it easily if negative words are thrown at me, it was so easy to manipulate my emotions and stir me towards provocation and anger, until God started showing me a new perspective to my relations with people, then I began to understand how to handle my emotions.

When people say mean things to you or treat you badly, trust me it is not about you, they are going through so much suffering on the inside that it begins to spill out of them, you shouldn't be mad at them, you should pray for God to touch their unhealed parts. You need to understand that no one can give what they don't have, you can't show what you have not experienced, people treat you the way they feel about themselves, to love another you must first love yourself, when you do not love yourself, it is impossible to love another, because you do not have the slightest idea how. People can only meet you as deeply as they meet themselves, the truth is most times criticism is born out of admiration, most times the people who say the worse things to and about you to others wish they were you, and they fact that they cannot be you drives them to the point of judging you and talking you down. Now when you let their words get to you or define you then you let them win and you give them your power.

You have to learn to ignore drama when you see it coming, learn to live above people's judgment, their opinion does not define you, when you dwell on their judgement then you let it define you. I use to say something to myself each time I hear hurtful things said to me, I tell myself am like rubber, every negativity bounces off and I just refuse to let words get to me or take root in my mind to weigh me down. I will tell you a story, when my elder sister got married a few years ago, naturally everyone was home for the wedding, it was the first time I was seeing a lot of our family friends in years, I knew I will hear a lot of side talks given the fact that my elder sister was getting married and I was next in line, the other tiny detail is that I was already a single mum, as prepared as I thought I was for all the side talks and questions, nothing prepared me for what I am about to share with you. A close family friend who I have come to see as an aunty of some sort sees me after so many years, I go over with my son to her, she bluntly says "Joy what happened with the father did he run away from you" For a minute I did not even know how to reply her, I took a deep breath and told her "no ma, it just did not work out" and I walked away. I was about to start letting it get to me and feel bad but I shook it off and wore her words like war paint and moved past it. I cannot explain why she was so insensitive but I am sure she didn't mean to hurt me. We live in a society where a lot of people still have misconceptions about single mums, I do not let it get to me. My experiences are meant to grow me and everything I have experienced have grown me into this woman I look in the mirror and I am proud I am becoming. I focus on the blessing and the lesson; I hold my head high because I am blessed and other people's words or opinion do not define me. Sometimes brutal honesty borders on you saying unkind words to people, it is a very thin line.

God has given you freewill that means your actions and decisions are yours to make, the consequences or rewards of those actions are yours to live with. If people understood this then we will all mind our businesses with the utmost respect for the persons business. People don't have to like the way you choose to look, dress, talk or act it is not their place to approve of what you do or want. The truth is your life is no one's business, what is everyone's business is being able to accept you for who you are regardless of how different you are from them. Loving you and being there for you if they choose to regardless of your choices, flaws or shortcoming, Jesus never judged all the people he encountered and helped to find their way in the Bible, all He did was save them by loving them not judging them. Love makes you see the world differently, when you have love in your heart, you have no place in your heart to be judgemental or unkind to anyone, you have no desire to rejoice at another person's wrong.

Don't take peoples actions towards you personal, it is okay to burn bridges or severe ties with people who pull you down with their association rather than build you up, they judge and criticise everything about you, love nothing about you, don't think you are good enough, when they hurt you with their words and fail to see how special or unique you are, you need to get up and walk, staying in such friendships or association is causing yourself more harm. It is ok to let go of toxic associations or any relationship that does not grow you. Your associations should bring out the best in you, letting negativity thrive around you will set you back in life and defile your mind, your mind is the garden where the seed of every dream that births your future is planted and if it is not watered with the right thoughts and words you end up living an empty and unproductive life.

I have come to realise that we are what we see in other people, our lives are a mirror giving us back our own reflections. What you see in people is in you that is why you recognise it when you see it, so be careful not to unmask yourself in the process of judging another. Do not let people's opinion of you define you, do not let people dictate your choices in life to you, people's opinions about your life only becomes a final verdict when you let. Simply ignore what doesn't serve you or grows you, do not spend your time brooding over what they say to or about you, your time is valuable spend it on the things that matter.

CHAPTER
16

LET GO OF THE PAST

*"We are all here for a reason stop being a prisoner of
your past and become the architect of your future"*
Unknown

The past to most people is their greatest enemy but the truth is the past is your greatest teacher. Everything you have been through has brought you to where you are today and it is taking you to where you are going in the future. The past is not meant to control you, it is meant to illuminate your present and prepare you for the future, your future.

Every single person on the planet has a past, some horrible, some not so horrible but you see your past does not define you, it is your choice to let it. Mistakes are teachers, we are meant to learn from them and move on from them. Your past is a part of you, it is a part of your journey, it is a part of your story, never be ashamed of it, whatever you went through was meant to grow you, whatever you did was because you probably didn't know better, that you feel some sort of remorse or shame shows that you know better now, you should own that past and see it as a tool to move forward, see the lessons as blessings to you and to people who you can share them with to learn from them.

Sometimes when we try to move on from the past, some people are going to keep digging it up or keep trying to remind us and torment us with it. Don't let that stop you from living your life, they torment you with it because they are still living in the past you have left behind long ago, they torment you or discuss your past because you have gone way above them and surpassed their expectation, you are now out of their reach and they need to pull you back down, do not let them , hold you head high and own your past , never deny it , yes that was you in the past but that isn't you anymore, the world cannot hold you to it, no one in his right senses should judge you by your past, you have moved way above it and your present is what matters. God didn't hold you to it, He forgave you and gave you a brand-new start, do not let anybody take you back to a place God has brought you out from.

We have all done things we are not proud of in the past, but it's easy to point fingers at other people, especially when we feel our past is a secret well starched away,

Jesus told the Pharisees when they wanted to stone the prostitute to death that he who has no sin cast the first stone, no one has a right to judge you by your past because we all have one, this was what Jesus was trying to teach the people. I have had instances when people have told other people they know me from way back, and the give stories or descriptions of me from who I used to be that totally contradicts who I am now, and I just smile and shake it off because that is not me, my growth game is on a constant rise, sometimes I get calls or meet people I knew from university and they expect me to still get excited about social outings that I will jump at years ago but now I find a total waste of time, because I have grown past my knowledge and understanding of life at the time and they won't just get it. You need to understand that if you want your change and grow to be complete, there are ties that need to be severed, bridges that need to be burnt, habits that need to be dropped, friends that need to go, in order for you to have that fresh start you desire, some of your associates from the past will not understand you are growing , they will revolt against it, hold it against you , try to pull you back because they do not understand why you want to be better or leave a more meaningful life, they will talk about you , try to defame your character with people, do not let that distract you from growing , do not entertain their behaviour or what they say, just brush it off, and keep growing and getting better proving everything they say wrong. Keep your change game so tight people can't keep up with it and gossips are constantly outdated with their news.

There are somethings that are better left in the past if you want a better present and a great future, the past can only hold you back if you let it, to become a better you, you must be able to move beyond who you used to be and what you used to know in order to be a better version of yourself.

Forgive yourself of your past, forgive people who have hurt you, it is a very important part of moving forward. When my father passed on years ago, I experienced the greatest form of cruelty, inhumanity and injustice dished out to my mum, sisters and I but for Gods intervention and protection it would have been a double tragedy. I saw people I have come to know as family turn against us, betray us, looting the much they could from us and didn't care what became of us. We were meant to be mourning my father but the horrific experiences we were taken through showed that no one cared, all they cared about was inheriting their late brother and putting his family on the street, after the burial I watched his brothers try on his clothes, wristwatches and shoes in excitement in his room as they came to pack his properties to the village, I was filled with so much hate, resentment and anger for so many years, I played back different scenes from that time over and over again in my head and each time I was more hurt than before, but it wasn't helping me it was polluting my mind and poisoning my heart, I was a prisoner of my hate for years until God open my eyes to the damage my negative emotions were doing to me. They say anger does more harm to the vessel than the person it is felt towards, actually the sad part is, it doesn't do anything to the person you feel it towards, that revelation made me understand feeling such negative emotions towards anyone is a totally waste of valuable time. So much has happened to me over the years that kept building up the mountain of anger and resentment that was eating me up by until God started putting me back together, He taught me one important ingredient and that was forgiving the past no matter how hard it is, it was hard letting go so I started a little exercise, I started calling up people from my past who have hurt me and those I felt I had hurt to make peace, starting from the trivial to the serious ones.

Gradually forgiving started feeling so good and easy, the peace was an amazing, love took over on the inside of me and I felt really warm, light and happy on the inside. It became so easy to let go of the bitterness of the past and forgive even the most grievous of offences. I forgave and let go of the past, as much as it was toxic and traumatic, I found a way to find the good and the lesson in it all, burnt some bridges in order to move forward with my life. Know this, you must close some doors or chapters completely in order to have a fresh start. I read somewhere that we meet people in our lives for different reasons, some are lessons and some are blessings, it is important to know lessons, learn from them, make peace with them and move on. Nothing is worth your peace of mind, if it won't matter years to come then you shouldn't lose sleep over it.

Life is so short and so frail, we need to understand the importance of forgiveness, forgiving yourself and forgiving people who have wronged you, just as I thought I had finished this chapter, I got news that a friend of mine passed and it was so devastating. We were not so close anymore because we had some discrepancies on lives choices and I had always hoped he would put his affairs in order at some point in the future, never for once did I think he was going to live this earth anytime soon, it was a shocking news and even more painful because I thought there was time, I thought he had time to grow into the fullness of who God has destined him to be and take responsibility for his life, the only peace I felt in all that chaos was the fact that I made peace with him three years earlier, if I hadn't I would have been so broken and full of regrets. It was a rude awakening for me that nothing is as important as the present, we are so busy pursuing the future, we forget what is important the gift of today and all that comes with it, our loved ones, family, purpose on earth and all. We keep holding on to the trivial, the mundane, the vain, the inconsequential, bitterness, pride at the expense of living today to its fullest. This late friend of mine had always been an ambitious person, the quest to be wealthy and influential overshadowed his love for everything else, his ambition always came first because of it he made some not-so-great choices and things did not end well.

Pride and selfishness play a very big role in ruining the future, pride specifically is one deadly factor that keeps us stuck in the past, waiting for an apology that will never come or might never come, we insist on being acknowledged or appreciated by someone who never will, and we just stay in that place like stagnant water and life keeps wasting away. Let go of the past, be satisfied with an apology you never got, be okay with the fact that no one acknowledges you, it doesn't matter what anyone does or does not do, just move past it and live your life, forget past hurts believe me it will not matter years down the line, whatever it is I can assure you, you will definitely heal and it won't matter anymore, some disagreements or situation are never resolved, the best resolution you get is giving yourself closure and moving on, that's what happens when you let go of the past.

Your past is gone, it is called the past, treat it as such, stop dragging it into your present because it will destroy your future. When you hold on to it, it's like holding on to a rope tightly that is hurting your palm but you just won't let it go, in the end all you get is pain and misery. Don't live in the past, you have already fought and won those battles, use your scars as lessons to teach and liberate others and not as shackles to hold yourself down.

CHAPTER
17

THE WORDS WE SPEAK ARE LIFE

"Your words are an extension of your thoughts; change your words you change your life" Louise Hay

Words are very powerful; our words define us and they reveal themselves as our lives unfold. Your words can build or destroy you, our confessions define our lives, are your utterances negative or positive? What are you telling yourself every day? The words we speak are life that means we must speak what we want into existence, no matter the situation we find ourselves.

When I was younger I spoke a lot of negative words to myself and believe me it manifested in my life, I was used to saying I am fat, I am broke, I am sick, my migraine headache , my ulcer, yes I went as far as owning rights and franchises to illnesses and became a slave to this infirmities for years until I discovered the power in the words I speak, it dawned on me that everything I was going through wasn't because I needed any form of special prayer or intervention, it wasn't because God had forgotten me or people were bewitching me from my village, it was the words I was speaking into my life , it was creating everything I was experiencing.

It was difficult to believe at first how mere words could be so powerful, until I tried speaking life and positive words to myself despite the reality I was confronted with daily and everything began to change instantly, life started becoming beautiful and stress free, I discovered I wasn't the unlucky one or the one God had forgotten, I just wasn't speaking the right words into my life.

What you tell yourself is what you experience, sometimes you might not experience it immediately but eventually you will, what you speak into people's lives or let people speak into your life take root, because the words were spoken and they were accepted. When people use negative words to describe you or speak to you, it doesn't matter if it's a joke, you must reject it immediately and counter it with positive words, do not let such words take root in your life. I have a friend who is quick to speak negative words jokingly when we are joking around, she would say "useless girl or yeye girl or you are a fool" jokingly that is, now she doesn't mean it but those words do not know that as they are sent forth they should be harmless because they person who spoke it is joking, when words are spoken they are sent forth and the only command they perform is what they are told whether you mean it or not, those words only have one mandate to fulfil the purpose they were spoken for so what I do is I counter the words with positive words smiling too , I say "am not useless oh am useful" and we will laugh some more, I replace negative utterances with positive words immediately.

As a parent the words you speak into the life of your children play a very vital role in their future, ever wondered why your child fails every examination and keeps doing poorly in school? Maybe it is because you call him or her block head all the time, ever wonder why you kid is finding it difficult to get his or her act together? Maybe it is because you have always referred to him or her as a useless child. As a spouse or a partner are you wondering why that relationship or marriage is just not working and everything is a mess, maybe is because of the words you speak into your partner's life every day. Words are powerful, you speak your circumstances into being. When God created the world, He spoke everything into being, just with the words that came out of His mouth, they were as He spoke them, the same applies to us as His children, we speak our lives, our circumstances and our future into being. If you knew the power in your words, you will never speak a negative word in your life again.

Speak life into your children's lives, even when they are falling back in their academics or misbehaving at home, look beyond that situation and speak what you want to see in their lives into their lives. Tell them they are blessed, they are intelligent, they are blessings to you, do not talk about what they are at the moment that you do not want, speak about who you want to see them become. When my son was three years old I started teaching him how to say positive words to himself, I made him t-shirts and on those t-shirts I wrote the following inscriptions, "I am good, I am kind, I am Obedient "I made him say those words every morning and every night before he went to bed, now he has added more affirmations of his own because he has come to understand the importance of speaking positive words to himself, he is nine now and those words have shaped my son's life, when I speak a negative a word he is quick to correct me, he says "mummy that is a negative word" I apologise and correct myself immediately. Speak what you want to see into the situations and people around you, don't keep complaining about what is wrong at work or in your relationship or marriage, don't keep grumbling about how badly someone is behaving, instead speak what you will want to see or experience , if you want to improve the relationship between you and your boss, then every day you should keep thanking God for giving you the best boss in the world, speak it until it becomes a reality, you have the power to speak what you want into being, that is why instead of saying you are broke, you should say I am rich, instead of saying you are sick you should say I am strong, because that is what you want your situation to be.

Every morning I wake and make declarations into my life to start my day, it puts me in the right frame of mind to start my day, I confession all the positive things I want to see in my life that day into existence before I step out in the morning. It builds my confidence and faith to conquer my day.

What type of words are you speaking into your life? Most of your curses roll off your own tongue with all the negative self-talk you dish out to yourself every day, words cast spells, the words you speak become the life you live, speak the right words into your life.

CHAPTER
18

IT IS BEST TO BE QUIET

'"When you can't control what is happening challenge yourself to control the way you respond to what's happening, that's where your power is" ... conscious collective

Silence saves you a lot of unnecessary apologies and troubles, most importantly silence protects you.

When you keep your affairs to yourself, the enemy doesn't know where, how and when to attack. When you understand that you do not need to have an answer to every word thrown at you or understand that you do not always have to have the final say, you have embraced wisdom and saved yourself a lot of stress and unnecessarily drama. Mastering the art of self-control is the true test of growth, you must be able to control your emotions and actions. Watch what you say, when you say it, and how you say it, words uttered cannot be taken back and most times it leads to years of set back and regrets.

The less you let out to people the better, when you have dreams and you are working on them, work in silence, let your achievements announce you, most times on social media you see people posting day in day out about ideas they are working on that haven't seen the light of day yet, in the end most times it remains just that, an idea, let your success announce you, do not kill your dreams prematurely because you could not be silent. Your affairs are your affairs and your business, you must keep it at that way, people do not have to know everything about you, it is funny this days how much people let strangers into their lives thanks to social media, when you go on Instagram or snap chat you see people post everything about their lives holding back nothing , including what they had for breakfast and lunch, who the just quarrelled with , who they just started dating, what they just bought and so on, every day they feel the need to inform total strangers about the private happenings in their lives, at some point when there is nothing more to share they gradually begin to post make believe daily itineraries to create a life that does not exist in real life on social media and then find themselves under pressure to keep up with the lie they have created, all these might have started with just one hashtag. It is ok to enjoy the social media spotlight if it is your thing but you need to know where to draw the line.

In your relationship with other people, it is important to understand that the ability to be calm and quiet in the midst of an argument is maturity, it also saves you a lot of drama. Anyone who knows me knows that being quiet in an argument is not one of my very strong points but in recent times I have learnt to be calm and quiet, still learning though, still a work in process, I have understood that not every attack deserves a response, sometimes I should sit it out and ignore especially when I know that getting into that argument or conversation will drain me rather than add any value to me. Most relationships fall apart because of the need for both parties to have the last word, you don't have to have the last word, it is okay not to have the last word, it doesn't make the aggressor right it just means you chose peace over the obsession to be right. It is important to listen, most times with most disagreements everyone wants to be heard no one wants to listen, listen to understand what the other persons point is. There is a quote that says "the problem with most relationships is partners listen to reply not to understand", this is the problem with communication, everyone wants to be heard no one is trying to listen. The same thing happens in our relationship with God, a lot of the problems we experience in life would have been avoided if only we listened and heard God giving us instructions about what was ahead of us. Our lives are so loud and noisy, we don't hear Him when He speaks, so we end making one avoidable mistake one after the other. You need to have one ear constantly tuned to hearing God because it helps you to make wise decisions. When you speak you are just repeating what you already know, but when you listen you learn more. The Bible says be quick to hear but slow to speak, there must be reason why God wants you to take your time to evaluate and think through things before you open your mouth to speak. Silence a priceless, it is wisdom, it improves your spiritual bond and relationship with God.

In your associations watch your conversations and watch what you say, the less you say, the less likely it is for you to get into trouble, know that that person you are trusting with your secret or someone else's secret is trusting someone else and soon enough your secret will not be a secret anymore, you could as well have gathered an audience and laid it on them.

I always felt better about an issue if I pour my heart out to a friend, it didn't take me long to realise it wasn't a very bright move, I will sit with my friends and lament over issues in my relationship or my life, it seemed okay at the time, because I was unburdening myself and I always felt better in the end, but the after effect most of the time wasn't worth the risk, for one I sometimes get to hear from someone else what I told another in confidence, in the end I was putting my relationship or life on the chopping block and giving people permission to see themselves as authorities in my relationship or life , I let them have opinions and also let them in on more than necessary. One day I sat down and thought about it really hard, I do not know anything about my confidant's private lives. They had issues too no doubt everyone does but they didn't sing about theirs like I sang about mine, so there was always a mystery surrounding them which commanded my respect, I began to understand my folly, I was the one who didn't know how to be discreet, I did not respect my privacy and if I didn't no one else would. I was not angry at my friends who took my issues out to other people because it was not their fault lesson learnt. I took responsibility for my actions and I began to find more resourceful ways to handle my issues or challenges, I only shared what was necessary with the very few people I could really confide in, having at the back of my mind that a smart person knows what to say, but a wise person knows whether or not to say it.

When you have a dream or project you are embarking on, put a lid on it, people do not have to know about it until it comes to full term, the more you talk about it , the higher the possibility of it being aborted before full term, some will try to discourage you , some will tell you is unachievable and give you convincing arguments why, some will instil fear in you , some will envy the fact that you have such a brilliant idea and will do all they can to either jeopardize it or steal the idea and make it happen before you, one day you will be sitting down and watch your idea pop up right in your face the only difference is it's no more yours , someone else has made it happened because you just couldn't keep your mouth shut. Discipline yourself to be okay with discussing your affairs with your father in heaven, then listen He will always talk to you and give you a way out of your situation. Silence will take you very far in life, when you do not say anything, no one knows what you are thinking, and no one can predict you, when people don't know what you are up to, they don't know what to attack, let your work announce you, be that person who tiptoes around the landmines of life that are avoidable just by being silent.

CHAPTER

19

THE ENEMY CALLED DEBT

Debt is born out of the lack of contentment, when you are always content with what you have at a particular time and you don't desperately wish what you do not have the resource to purchase or have at any point in time you can never find yourself in debt.

I was a slave to debt for so many years of my life, at the point am writing this book I am still paying off debts I have accumulated over time , it started with people who wanted to sell their goods to me telling me they trusted my credibility , then you take all you want with the projection that you will pay later and you plan on funds you have not seen yet, it was working out pretty well at first and I saw there was no harm in it everyone else was doing it, so gradually I started buying things are needed and then those that I wanted and thought I needed which in the end I found out I would have done just fine without. The debts began to grow, the means to pay began to thin out, the calls and text for payment started becoming bothersome and stressful, sometimes at 5 am in the morning, I had headaches and anxiety because of my creditors, and the sad part is you cannot get angry even if they call you at 2 am because you are owing them money, no wonder the Bible says the borrower is a slave to the lender. Once it got really bad, I will tell God "please if you help me get out of this debt I will never owe again" He always came through for me, before you know it, I'm out of that and into another, especially when friends need to sell stuff to me, they were okay with me paying anytime but anytime soon becomes I need my money now and then the circle begins again. That was not all, sometimes I want to get a project or problem solved and the urgency would make me borrow money from friends with the promise to pay back at a particular time, but my projections had failed a couple of times and I don't get to keep my word. One day I woke up and I had all this messages from people I owed and I was ashamed and angry at myself , I asked myself how did I get here ? most of the people I owed ,I didn't have any business owing, the things I bought or needed money for could have honestly waited, I found out it was just indiscipline on my part, I also noticed that I had become used to it and became so comfortable I didn't even know how bad it had gotten until that morning, because some of those projects could have waited, some of these needs could have waited, there wasn't any urgency, my impatience just felt like those projects and needs were urgent.

I knelt down wrote a long list of the people I owed and asked God for forgiveness and ask for the grace and discipline to upset every debt and live within my means. From that moment I would not buy if I couldn't pay cash, I would not pursue a project if I didn't have the cash. The Bible says a borrower is a slave to the lender and in all honesty that is so true, when you are indebted to people you are in a certain kind of bondage, your life is controlled by your creditors, they can call you at any time, odds hours and you cannot get upset because they have a right to, the worst part is you will lose sleep, you will be stressed and sometimes you might even make a lot of bad calls in the desperation to pay what you owe.

I have a very dear friend who made some bad business calls and went into very huge debts with so many people running into millions of naira, that she is still alive and the stress didn't kill her it is the grace of God, she got death threats, threats to family's safety, she was invited to the police station so many times, served legal documents , it was a traumatic experience for her, she ran into this depth of debt because she was upsetting her principal debt with funds other trusting clients were paying her for their own transactions, so she was getting deeper into more debt because for one her principal was accruing huge interest, at the end of the day she was owing so many people and her principal debt was far from being paid, she lost credibility with most of her clients she has built trust with over the years , it was a very sad situation happening to a very good hearted and hardworking lady , all of these happened because she made some bad calls and projected on invisible monies in the future. That is how debt traps you, you are optimistic that you have money coming in, forgetting that you also have issues and needs coming in in the future that will need the attention of that money, also you are in a hurry to get things that can wait till you are able to afford them, you find yourself prioritising the needful things as far as you are concerned over your debt, in the end your life is stressed, you are deprived of sleep, you cannot save and most importantly you lose integrity with people, which is a very hard thing to build back. I have learnt to be content with what I have, if I cannot afford to buy a new dress or shoe with cash right now then I do not need it, I will plan towards getting it in cash, if I cannot afford a car right now, I won't take a juicy payment plan I will work towards saving up for it. Most times they things we go into debt for are not things we really need that is the sad part. Think about it, most of the things you find yourself in debt over the things you would have lived comfortably without. Debt is a silent killer, a lot of men have died of heart failure, from huge debts they had and had no means of paying, because they have given their family a false life for so long, most of the debts are accumulated from the luxury cars, huge mansions, extremely expensive schools and extravagant holidays they have provided their family over time, the need to be seen as an adequate provider makes a lot of men go overboard, when they can no longer live with the shame and disappointment, the pressure from the banks and threats from money lenders finally kills them and their family is left with debts to pay. They are sadly left to deal with a situation they did not create while struggling to survive. Their lives Change in an instant, just because one man made a bad call.

I think for me this is one of the biggest life's lesson I had to learn, you must plan your life, have a financial plan, don't live your life in the spur of the moment, develop a saving culture, no matter what save a percentage of your earnings, plan ahead for your children's education and your future, do not spend your future on frivolities today. Sometimes when am cleaning out my house and getting rid of things we do not need; I see a lot of stuff I bought that I didn't necessarily have to buy and that explained my years of financial struggle. Living in debt is an addiction, it becomes a lifestyle, you become used to it, you see nothing wrong with it and it begins to drag you into a stressful life of constant lack little by little, a lot of people who appear rich and wealthy are actually living in poverty from the cars, to the clothes to the holidays to the house that are not completely paid for, different banks, financial houses, vendors and loan sharks are pursuing them day in day out for loans the really didn't have to take.

Know this your peace of mind is priceless and a life of debt will take it away from you, learn to live within your means, be discipline in your spending, you do not have to have everything you want, focus on what you need, and work towards the luxuries you desire, they will come in time but until then do not drown yourself in debts in a hurry to make it happen. Debts will take away your dignity and your future, I learnt my lesson the hard way, for years I didn't have a single savings and my earnings were never sufficient because once it came in, debts took the better part of it , I could not afford vacations or pay for emergency bills, like medical bills or light bills sometimes because I never had any money saved up. I had to let God work in and through me to get out of that life. Experiencing what sleeping peacefully meant without worrying that the next call is from a creditor and being able to save and plan vacations was a blessing. Living in debts destabilises your whole life, the pressure, stress and anxiety make it almost impossible to function or focus on building your future, day in day out, your time keeps slipping away while you are running up and down looking for ways to upset the debts.

You might be telling yourself what I owe isn't much and I always pay, well that is how it starts, and gradually it begins to grow on you and brings you to a point that it becomes a circle you are constantly stuck in. Make a conscious discussion today, be content at all times, save for the future and discipline yourself to have control over the urge to go overboard, you are not in competition with anyone just because everyone is buying it, owning it and wearing it doesn't mean you must enslave yourself to debt to join the band wagon. Be wise, protect your peace of mind, a mind without peace leads to an unproductive life.

CHAPTER
20

BE A SOLUTION

Take your life seriously, work hard at being successful, be a solution provider not a constant help seeker, nobody wants to associate with a liability no matter how kind-hearted they are after a while you become a burden and your visits or calls become a bother. When my dad passed on, a lot of our family friends made promises to our family to be there for us and provide whatever we need, some even offered to give us scholarships and pay for our education, months down the line all those promises faded away, everyone had returned to their lives and we were left to face the reality of it, except for a few amazing families that have stood behind us through thick and thin up until today. Right from then even as a young girl, I knew I wanted to become someone of value so that no one treated me like a liability.

Aspire to add value to people's lives, when you are able to add value to people's lives, you will naturally earn the respect of people, the Bible says the gift of a man makes way for him before kings and princes, when you are a person of value it brings you before great men, they will seek your counsel, wealth becomes an added bonus. Live a life of impact, ask yourself how you can add value to the world you live in and not the other way around, what do you think God has deposited in you that your world needs, you need to find it and put it to good use. I read somewhere that in life you only have two choices, which is love and fear, the choice you make determines the life you create, choose love, do not let fear take over your loving heart, it will stop you from giving your life meaning.

Don't play the waiting game, don't wait for your finances to get better or your relationship or the economy to change, nothing will change except you get up and make a conscious effort to change and be better, decide to start today, decide to be better, it will start a domino effect and with time your life will be better, soon your world will be better also. Being a solution in your world most times isn't about money, sometimes it's about what you have to say, the song you sang, the smile you gave away, the hug you gave, the food you made, the prayer you offered, you don't have to make all the money in the world to be a solution to your world. At this very moment I sit and I am writing this chapter of this book, I have a long list of bills that need to be paid, I am still trusting God for money to print this book and get it to you to read it. The difference now is I have changed my perspective to life, instead of being depressed, anxious and worried about how to sort all these problems out, I am focused on adding value to my world. I am focus on using the gift God has given me to bless my generation, I have decided to seek the kingdom first, I have come to understand that all I need to excel in life and be successful is inside of me, I just need to act, anyone who writes knows it takes a lot of concentration, peace and creativity to write, I have chosen to have that mind-set in the midst of all my storm. If you are reading this book right now know it is a true testimony that you have it in your hand right now shortly after I wrote it, all it takes is the special grace of God, the right mind set, believing in yourself, taking action, finding your calling and your purpose and working towards actualising it is the key to a fulfilled and successful life.

I was always governed by fear in the past, I never go through with anything for fear of being wrong or failing, I have wasted precious time and the potential God has deposited in me, other people have exploited my gifts because I never got up or had the courage to put it to work, when my learning process began, I rose above the fear and today I can't explain the feeling it is better experienced, all I know is now I feel like my life now truly counts for something. This book is being written because someone somewhere needs it and I am glad I had the courage to write it, someone somewhere needs what God has put in you and is asking you to do

, stop hesitating, you have waited enough, choose love over fear and get to work, make your existence count.

Your value is in your calling, your calling is in the things that excite you , the things you are passionate about, most people spend years running after different businesses and career choices, unfulfilled, unhappy, unsuccessful and broke, until you fall in line with your calling , what God has placed in you is a gift to touch humanity and make a difference, when you yield to this calling the value God has placed in you will emerge and people will see it, recognise it, respect it and yearn for it. When you focus on your gift and build your life around it , life becomes stress free, your rat race for financial freedom ends, because you are doing what you love for the right reasons, you are touching lives with that love and in turn God blesses the works of your hands, it's a universal law, we get what we give, when you give of yourself, empty yourself to bless others out of love, no matter what your career, vocation or art is , God blesses you tremendously in return, for every life you touch with your work that appreciates or blesses you , heaven responds to it.

You might not know how many lives you heal or touch with what you do , but believe whatever it is you do it has an adverse effect on people's lives, whether you are a caterer, doctor, lawyer, politician, artist, dancer, footballer, comedian, mechanic, cleaner, whatever it is you do, you add value to people s life. If you are reading this book right now and you are still figuring out what you want to do with your life or you are still sitting at home waiting for a big break, get up right now and make your life count for something, turn the tables, drop that list you make every morning of people you want to call for help, change the statuesque start being a person of value, anywhere you find yourself think about how you can add value to people not how they can help you, always think of what you can give , what you can offer not what you can get, they more you give of yourself , the more you will receive. The secret to success is putting your gift to work, finding your role in this world and playing it, finding your place in humanity and occupying it.

CHAPTER
21

MAKE YOUR LIFE COUNT

Life painfully but true is short, you never know when your time is up, make the time you have count, live a life of purpose so when your time is up you would have truly lived, leaving an indelible mark and a legacy for generations to come.

We are most times carried away by those things that do not matter, the mundane things, wealth, riches, fame and the likes, we take for granted the things that matter, family, love, life, purpose, in the end we waste a beautiful and priceless opportunity to live. It is true the say the greatest talents and gifts are buried in the cemetery, so many people leave this earth without living out their life s purpose. A friend of mine passed away, he was less than 40, he had always had tall dreams, always wanted to be wealthy, always wanted to be famous, that was his driving force, those were the reasons that drove his passion daily, I keep thinking if he only knew he had a little over 30 years to live on this earth, would he have done things differently? I have a strong feeling he would have. I sat down and ask myself in sober reflection, if my time was up today, will I say I have lived a full life and accomplished the purpose God brought me into this world for? I was brutally honest with myself, my answer was far from a yes but not an outright no, but in the end it wasn't a sure yes, I was somewhere in the middle hanging like a yoyo in between the yes and the no parts, it brought me to a painful realisation that I have taken my life for granted most of the years I have lived so far and let a lot of years go by without nothing but mere excuses why I was not living the life God intended for me or impacting my generation or birthing my dreams or putting my gifts to good use. It was a wakeup call for me, I felt a sense of urgency to get things going and get it right, and it became my paramount goal to make sure God did not regret creating me.

One woman who inspires me so much is Joyce Meyers, if you are familiar with her story, you will know she had been through hell as a young girl but she didn't let it define her instead she rose above her past hurt and made a decision to use her experience to help other people through her ministry, that's not all she goes all over the world bringing hope to a dying world, spreading love and putting a smile on the face of millions of people especially in impoverished countries.

Mother Teresa is another remarkable woman I admire, she has more or less been immortalised for her selfless service to humanity, she lived her whole life sharing the love of Christ to people that have been rejected and abandoned by the society. When I read how she ran a home for leprous people, where she shared the Gods love with them and helped them find peace, joy and redemption in whatever religion they understood God in the final days of their journey on earth I was so touched, can you imagine someone spending time with people who are called untouchables, whose fates have been sealed and still letting them know they are loved? It's amazing, I read a quote by her once which said the only thing, she asked of God was for her to be a pencil in His hands through which He wrote his message of love to the world and that was what she spent her whole life being, Gods instrument of love.

When Jesus said seek ye first the kingdom and all other things would be added to you, He meant live a life of service, kingdom service, a life of purpose, a life that is driven by love for humanity, a life focused on putting your gifts to work to fulfil your calling and all the other things you desire, money, wealth, promotion and so on will naturally follow towards you. There is nothing more rewarding and fulfilling than living a life of selfless service to humanity. Think about this long and hard, when your time on earth is done, what will you be remembered for? What will the world thank you for? What legacy would you have left behind? Start now make your life count.

I wrote in an earlier chapter, we all have roles to play on this stage of life, that is why we are here, there is a purpose, a reason for your existence, fulfilling that purpose should be your foremost dream in life, find it, immerse yourself in it and make it a reality, don't just exist, live a life with meaning, stand for something, live for a cause, make every waking moment count.

CHAPTER
22

BE GRATEFUL ALWAYS

"Gratitude is the gate way to Gods provision"
Steven Furtick

Gratitude is a very powerful force; it is a force that can change your life in the instant. If you start listing the things you are grateful for now, it begins to make you feel good, feel blessed and then you begin to fell truly grateful, this is the fastest way to change whatever circumstance you find yourself in or get answers to your prayers. Most times we are locked in a circle of challenges because of ingratitude. We get so carried away worrying about what we do not have, we forget all the amazing gifts around us.

Being thankful for the life you have brings you into the life you desire, gratitude opens doors, it unlocks heaven, God loves a grateful heart, and your gratitude moves him to do more, the more you are grateful the more good you are ushering into your life. Always find something to be thankful for especially when you are going through a hard time, it might look like there is nothing to be thankful for, but once you start with being thankful for the air you breathe, every other blessing will begin to come to you. Whenever you are confronted with challenges, learn to fight back with thanksgiving. If you are ill thank God for the rest time he is giving your body and the gift of pain which made you know you were ill in the first place , thank Him for the air that goes into your lungs, if you are broke thank God for the times you have had money and the things you were able to buy with it , thank him for giving you an opportunity to know what it feels like not to have and appreciate Him for the times you had money , if you are jobless, thank Him for the free time He has put on your hands getting you rested before your job comes. Find a blessing, something to be thankful for in the midst of every challenge, focus on the good, so your heart can stay grateful, it creates a rippling effect that transforms your life. If you want something more you have to be grateful for the one you have now, the Bible says whatever you ask of the father, believe you have received giving thanks to the father, when you give thanks as though you have received what you ask God for, it moves Him to make it available to you speedily.

I read a book by Rhonda Byrne called The Secret, the book talks about how our thoughts creates our reality, it also talks about the two most powerful forces that activates our blessings, love and gratitude, I went on to buy her books The Power and The Magic (two wonderful books), the latter talks about how gratitude is a game changer and the fact that it is a key to the life we desire. She has a 27-day gratitude exercise in the book that will help the reader cultivate an attitude of gratitude by applying gratitude to everyday life. Each day she has a new exercise, something in your life to be thankful for from the most obvious things to the things we overlook every day, but one thing I found constant everyday was the fact that every morning you have to list ten things you are grateful for and then at night hold a gratitude stone and think about your whole day and be grateful for the things that you experienced but you must close your eyes and really feel the gratitude, be truly grateful from the inside. The first time I carried out the 27-day gratitude exercise like one unbelievable miracle everything began to change for the better and the things I stressed about in the past started coming to me with ease. I repeat the exercise each time I am overwhelmed with life and it starts getting difficult to stay thankful, the moment I start, by the second day things begin to change for the better, over the years it helped me cultivate an attitude of gratitude no matter the situation I find myself because I discovered that my life was better and beautiful whenever my heart was filled with gratitude. These days some people don't understand the dimension of my gratitude and joy even in the midst of challenges, but that is because I have gotten to a point where I feel unconditional gratitude, I do not need a reason to be grateful, the more things look bleak the more grateful I am and, in the end, things always change for the best.

You might be saying , she is not going through what I am going through what does she know, the truth is as long as you are not dead and you still wake up every morning, it can't be that bad, because you are still breathing that is a good place to start, that is enough reason for you to be grateful to God, as long as he gives you another day, it means He is not through with you yet and that means it is not the end of your story, but how that story goes is up to you , whether it gets worse or better depends on your attitude because your attitude determines your altitude. If you keep complaining and murmuring things will keep getting worse, complaining means you are asking for more of the same situation but if you decide to choose a better path and keep thanking God for life, He will be moved to make things turn around for your good. Gratitude will shift you to a higher frequency and you will attract better things into your life.

CHAPTER
23

CONQUERING YOUR FEARS AND ACTIVATING YOUR DESTINY

"Fear is only as deep as the mind goes"
"Underneath your fears lie great opportunities"

Fear is a crippling emotion, when it cripples your mind it can hold you back for everything. I know because I have been a victim of this emotion for so many years, I would have achieved a lot more that I have by now but for the gripping hands of fear, I had the fear of everything, fear of failure, fear of being wrong, fear of been laughed at, fear of addressing people, fear of the unknown whatever other fear there is name it I had it, I was even afraid of being in the dark alone, funny isn't it? Yes, it is true and a lot of people out there suffer from the same bondage called fear holding them back from breaking forth into their true calling and revealing themselves to the world. Know that as long as fear holds you down you can never step into your destiny.

Most times your worse fear stands right in front of your life's purpose, once you conquer that fear you activate your calling and destiny. For as long as I can remember I have always had stage fright, when I have to address a crowd of people, even a handful I become so anxious and unsure of myself, on the other hand I am a very eloquent speaker with so much inside to share, I have been writing for years but I have never completed any of my works, because in the middle or just when I start writing, I start with the what ifs and then I abandon ship. It took me conquering my fear to write this book and even then, there were times during the process of writing and publishing that I had second guessed this work and thought of quitting it but the difference this time is I know my calling and life's purpose now and I knew I had two choices either to feed my faith or feed my fear, the prior will move me forward, the latter will keep me running in circles living an unfulfilled life. Whatever dream you have that scares you is the very dream you should pursue, think about this for a minute, I had anxiety feelings from the day I contacted the publishers to the day this book was unveiled publicly, I can write this because I know how I feel anytime I am working on a project and I know how I feel right now even as I am writing, the difference is I didn't give up or let the feeling subdue me and stop me from achieving my dream this time. The only thing standing between you and your goal is the thoughts you feed yourself on the inside as to why you cannot achieve it, and these thoughts emanate from a place of fear. Fear exists only in your mind, it is not real, but the attention you give it begins to concretise it in the decisions you make about your life. When you feed it, it begins to birth feelings of insecurity, indecision, low self-esteem and inactivity Your life's purpose is why you are here, it is your calling, it is what validates your creation, it is what fulfils you as an individual, that is the value you add to humanity, if you don't find it and activate it you will keep going round in circles, living a life of struggle. From personal experience I can tell you for a fact that once you find your calling and key into your life's purpose you activate your destiny and cease to live a life of struggle. My Pastor once said that when the road is not known, time is wasted, it is so true, we spend years struggling with one business or life path until we make that brave decision to confront the fear that stands right in front of the dream you have buried deep inside you, you always know it, you feel it, you can tell this is what you are meant to do but you might be too scared to walk the path and then you choose to walk familiar and easier paths that are leading you nowhere.

You gain strength and confidence each time you stare fear in the face, I have learned that fear limits you from achieving your dreams, it acts as blinders to your life's purpose. Have the courage to believe in yourself, your potentials, your abilities and your self-worth, this will allow you to achieve your goals and dreams. Don't let fear and insecurity stop you from trying new things, believe in yourself and find the courage to take that life changing step into activating your destiny. Know that fear will always be around to tell you what you cannot do, it is up to you to face your fears and tell yourself you can, the sooner you make that decision the sooner you embark on the precise journey of your life into a glorious future.

CHAPTER
24

LIFE IS BEAUTIFUL

"Don't waste your time chasing butterflies, when you mend your garden, the Butterflies will come" Mario Quintana

This is the heart of the matter, the sum of all the lessons, my daily mantra, life is beautiful, that is how I see life, everything is beautiful, there is beauty all around me, I refuse to see anything else, a lot of people think I live in a bubble and have refused to grow up or see all the harsh realities of life. I have a friend who told me a long time ago, that the fact that I am always happy and optimistic about life annoys him, he said life is so depressing he doesn't know what I see or experience that makes me happy all the time. I started giving him this long talk about happiness being a choice regardless of whatever we are going through but I knew I was hitting a brick wall, somethings you cannot talk people into understanding, they have to decide, they have to choose to open the eye of their minds to see and experience life differently. Today they are a lot of people living like that, people who let their environment and circumstances control their view point about life. You need to create the world you want to see and live in with the thoughts you choose to dwell on and what you choose to hear and feel, it is a choice, being happy is a choice and it comes from the inside not from the outside, life is only as good as your mind set, if you are happy and content on the inside the outside will naturally follow suit.

If you are not doing what you love you are wasting your time, make your passion your means of livelihood, doing what you love brings fulfilment. You need a fresh start? Clean the slate and start all over, it's never too late to start over, if you are not happy about yesterday, try something different today, don't stay stuck, do better. Know your strength and your potential and guard it, channel it towards your calling , put them to good use if not someone else will exploit it , be careful, there are people who will be drawn to your strength, people who seek to harness it and use it to their own benefit, they will want to own it and own you , keeping you from growing into who you are meant to become, they will have you eating from the palms of their hands and whatever will ensure your independence or your success they will subtly frustrate or sit on , under the guise of looking out for you or having your interest at heart , ask God for grace to discern this type of people and stay far away from them.

Fall in love, fall in love hard but make sure who ever he or she loves and values you much, that losing you scares them. Make sure they support your dreams and goals and are the leader of your cheer leading team. You would know if it is real, because you would not have a second guess or wonder about anything, the actions will match the words. When it is love, he or she will trust and respect you, you will matter and every detail about you will be important to him or her. Never settle for the next best thing, never give up on love, when you are ready love will find you.

Strive to be the best you can be, never be in competition with anyone, the only one you can be in competition with is the person you were yesterday. It doesn't matter what the trend is, what the world is crazy about, what the majority are after, dare to stand out, be your own person, do what makes you happy, wear what makes you comfortable, focus on what is important to you, don't be under pressure to please anyone or proof anything to anyone, the only person you have to proof anything to is yourself. Do not make other people authorities on your life, it is your life, it should be your choice because those choices you make you will be responsible for.

No matter what life throws at you get up and fight, fight through it, if it looks like plan A is not working, move to your back up plan, if that doesn't work move to the backup of the backup plan, whatever you do always make sure you have a plan and giving up shouldn't be one of them. You have to keep going no matter what, persistent and determination pays off eventually. Be prepared for the opportunities God is bringing your way, more importantly be sensitive to times and seasons, it is said that success is opportunity meeting preparation, prepare yourself for the future you want, take courses, read books, acquire knowledge about any and everything, know that no knowledge is wasted, train yourself in character and discipline your spirit, be ready when opportunity comes knocking, recognise it, take it and make the best of it.

Keep your eye on the ball, avoid distractions and anything that will pollute your spirit. Stay away from people who constantly bring up your past to crush your spirit, don't let them pull you back to a place you have left a long time ago, do not engage them in their toxic drama, choose to ignore and focus on associations that grow you and feeds your spirit right.

Do not settle for less, you deserve the best of the best, you are special, you are one of a kind and deserve all the best life has to offer, never ever settle for the next best thing or the available. Know who you are, you are royalty, you are divinity made in Gods own image, who shouldn't be talked down to or abused in anyway, you are royalty so you must treat yourself as one. Love yourself, know you are beautifully and wonderfully made, every single thing about you is perfect and needs no modification, I watched a motivational video by Aston Kutcher, he said "be sexy, the sexiest thing in this world is being smart, thoughtful, kind and generous, everything else is just crap that people try to sell to you to make you feel less of yourself". All the labels, plastic surgeries, trends, cars, parties, jewelleries, fame and class don't make you beautiful, beauty is innate, when your inside is beautiful, your outside will be beautiful too. Be kind regardless of how people are, they are fighting their own battles, look for the good in everyone you see and respect their journey, sometimes it is tough to focus on the good especially when people keep dishing one mean episode after another, when you have it at the back of your mind that they are fighting their own demons and it has nothing to do with you, you will easily overlook their excesses and focus of the good.

Trust your journey and trust the process your journey takes you through, everything you are going through good or bad is grooming you for the future you have always desired. Everyone you meet through life have roles they play in your life, doesn't matter whether they encourage or torment you , one thing is sure they are pushing out of your comfort zone and moving you closer and closer to your destiny. This book is a reality today because God brought a very exceptional and amazing woman who motivated and propelled me towards my calling. Sometimes God brings people your way to help you find yourself, some might help you in love, others through the horrible experiences they take you through. I read a story once about a young lady who went through the worse kind of sexual abuse from her uncle and physical abuse from her father, one of the stories she told that hit me hard , was about getting pregnant at 13 by the uncle who was abusing her, he took her to a local chemist , who forcefully spread her out and began to use a sharp object inside of her to terminate the pregnancy, in her words the pain was incomprehensible she screamed so hard she could barely recognise her voice , eventually he finished and she must have passed out, she was kept there for three days, fed once a day and giving just paracetamol, the heart breaking part was her family didn't even notice she was gone, she was helpless, when her uncle took her back home, he threatened her not to say a word to anyone, now this was just one of her many horrible experiences as a child, fast forward years later, she is using her pain and scars to encourage other young people who have been hurt, she is showing immense love to broken and helpless people around her, preaching the message of healing and self-love, I was drawn to her because she has channelled her pain positively , she chose to love regardless of all the loveless experiences she has had. No matter what hand you have been dealt in life, choose to be right by people, use your pain to heal the world.

Be wise, the world can be treacherous, be generous with your profit but do not spend your investment in the name of generosity just to impress people, in the end the same people who will celebrate and applaud you for your generosity, will mock you when all your money is gone. I heard someone say, when you are sweet the world will lick you but when you are bitter, they world will throw you away, a rich man has many friends, success has many friends, the only problem is they are not friends, they are fair weather associates who will leave you out in the cold when you are down, don't gamble your future way just for a moment of fame and popularity, be patient and work hard, your time will come.

Do not let people dictate or set the pace for your life, don't be pressured by the norm, break free from the mould and dare to do big things. Choose to live life don't just exist, don't wake up one morning with regrets of the things you could have done but never did or the places you would have gone you never went or the words you could have said and you never said, live your life on your own terms, love unconditionally, be kind to all.

THE END

www.ingramcontent.com/pod-product-compliance
Lightning Source LLC
Chambersburg PA
CBHW070718160726
47998CB00024BA/1857